WOMEN CRIMINALS IN INDIA

WOMEN CRIMINALS IN INDIA

Sociological and Social Work Perspective

By

A. Thomas William

A.J. Christopher

ANMOL PUBLICATIONS PVT. LTD.

NEW DELHI - 110 002 (INDIA)

ANMOL PUBLICATIONS PVT. LTD.
4374/4B, Ansari Road, Daryaganj
New Delhi - 110 002
Ph.: 23261597, 23278000
Visit us at: www.anmolpublications.com

Women Criminals in India
© Author(s)

First Published 2004

ISBN 81-261-1601-3

[All rights reserved. No part of this publication may be reproduced, stored in a retrieval system or transmitted, in any form or by any means, mechanical, photocopying, recording or otherwise, without prior written permission of the publisher.]

PRINTED IN INDIA

Published by J.L. Kumar for Anmol Publications Pvt. Ltd., New Delhi - 110 002 and Printed at Mehra Offset Press, Delhi.

Contents

Contents

Preface

In recent time the number of criminal offences committed by females has increased at a much higher rate than the number of crimes committed by males. In India it is estimated that the female crime rate has increased by 362.53% for a period from 1971 to 1990. Socially the crimes committed by females are considered more serious when compared with the male criminality since the role played by a women as mother, wife, caretaker and more to say a central figure in the family. Her role is very crucial and significant and hence female criminality is considered to be more dysfunctional.

The various dimensions of women and crime has recently been developed into a broad field of research in the areas of Social work, Sociology, criminology and women studies. Starting from Otto Pollak (1950), Smith (1962), Sutherland (1970), Adler (1975), etc. from abroad and in India Sharma (1965), Ahuja (1969), Nagla (1982), Rani (1983), Khosh (1986), Joseph (1992), Saxena (1994), etc. are notable researchers who could contribute to the knowledge of women and crime. For the past two decades the topic of women and crime has began to attract much attention because of new interest in women and development.

It was Rajkumari Sharma who is one of the early women in India who has done research on women criminality (1965) in Uttar Pradesh. A systematic presentation in book form on female offenders in India was done by Ram Ahuja (1969). Various sponsoring angencies like Bureau of Police Research and Development, Ministry of Social Welfare, Social Defence, etc., have created much attention on the subject.

However, it is a fact there are only few researchers who could systematically and scientifically approach the problem. Hence in the present study an effort has been made to comprehesively understand the socio economic background, cause, nature and the pattern of the crime in relation with the socio-cultural antecedents. The consequences are measured at four levels viz, on the criminal herself, children, family and society. The study also extends its scope beyond the prison by enquiring about the details of their husbands', network of friends and relatives in the criminal context, childhood criminal records, family of orientation and family of procreation, facilities and treatment available in the prison and their future plan after release.

It is hoped that these objectives may increase our understanding inorder to decrease the women enter into the system by offering suitable preventive and rehabilitative measures.

A thorough enquiry has been made with the structured pretested carefully made interview schedule covering each and every minute aspects mentioned in the objectives. It is an explorative study which explains the socio-economic conditions, nature and pattern of crime, causes, consequence on individual family, children and society, particulars regarding family of orientation, family of procreation, details of husbands, facilities and treatment available in the prison and their future plan after release.

The women criminals housed in two prisons in Tamilnadu viz. Vellore and Madurai were contacted through the prison officials. It was a historic event, that for the first time a male researcher entering into these women prisons.

Though there were initial inhibition the researcher took them to the confidence and he successfully collected the data with much overwhelming cooperation from the inmates. This was possible because of the rapport established with the respondents before every interview. It took four to five hours per inmate. All the inmates both convicted and under trials were included for the study. Moreover personal observation, discussion with the prison officials, especially with the welfare officers helped the researcher to understand in depth about the subject.

There are ten chapters have elaborately been discussed in this present book.

The chapter I introduces the subject, the background, need for the present study, the various objectives and methodology. In methodology the universe and sampling frame are explained in detail. The tool for data collection and the technique of data collection with operational definition of various terminologies used and the chapterisation are covered.

In the chapter II the literature has been reviewed with the various of crime, historical perspectives major theories meant for female criminality and how applicability is done for male crime theories to women offenders. The nature of the women crime is dealt with utmost care taking into account the various women criminality researchers which also includes the recent trends in the nature of women criminals. A thorough enquiry into the empirical studies has been made with the following important aspects such as profile, family background, victim/clients, acceptance of crime and accomplice. The trends of crime in abroad and inland have also been mentioned.

The reason for women enter into criminal system have been examined with the specific headings of economical factors, social factors, sexual relation, status of women, changing social roles, psychological causes, premenstrual period, environmental factors, impact of urbanization and modernization. Research studies on women prisoners, rehabilitation measures, role of social work in prison setting, case work, counselling and additional skills required for correctional social worker to deal with women criminal are also discussed in detail. The various literature on women criminals suggest that only little attention paid to the area of extending beyond the prison and rehabilitative measure.

The chapter III speaks about the personal profile of the respondents such as age, education, marital status, occupation, monthly income, caste, religion and domicile. These particulars are crossed with the type of crime committed for comparative analysis and which gives a clear picture to understand the criminals better. The criminals are classified into five patterns of types viz., murder–non murder, crime with victims–non victims, crime against person, property and morality, convicts –under trails, long-term short-term prisoners. These five patterns were compared and crossed with the personal profile. The chapter IV deals with the family of orientation where in a background about the partial treatment, residential description, quarrel some nature in the family, sibling position, financial difficulties are elaborately interrogated and this makes every reader to have an indepth analysis about the root cause problem and how their family environment sown and grown the criminal seed in the mind when the criminals were children.

Family of procreation is the another field of battle how these women were suffered and how the criminal seed manured and irrigated–are discussed in the V chapter, Marriage particulars-legal or illegal, frequency of marriage for the women and their husbands, age at marriage, illtreatment by the members of family of procreation, conflict, details about husband and illegal relationship of the women and/or husbands' are extensively dealt with. It is an awful fact that illegal relationship plays an important role in the life of those women as vast percentage of either women or their husbands had illegal contact and these condition make them to revolt to antisocial activities.

In the chapter VI the causation was discussed with various variables. Added to that childhood criminal behaviour, acceptance and false implication details, distribution according to crime and district wise, age at first crime committed, victim, relationship with the criminals, weapon used, frequency and nature of crime committed, details regarding surrender and arrest are also discussed.

The consequences are the most important part the research. The perceived and/or experienced consequence of the subject are studied so as to suggest future rehabilitation programmes. In the same direction the consequences are also measured using the five point scales. Consequence at the four levels viz., themselves, children, family and society are discussed with carefully selected ten statements each and tabulated in the chapter VII.

In the chapter VIII the prison life, punishment period, visits by the friends and relatives, the effect of prison life, facilities available, future plan after release and acceptance in the family and society are discussed. The future plan of the respondents suggests us how the fallen women are endangered to future risk. There is also an interesting matching done with the nature of crime committed and their families' acceptance. The difficulties as they perceived after release and help expected from Government and other agencies are also covered in this chapter. For many, the prison life seems to be miserable and the poor facilities of food, dress, lack up privacy and the lack of recreation also experienced by them.

In the summary and suggestion in the IX chapter the objectives of studies is systematically taken and accordingly summary is given. Starting from socio cultural antecedents, causes, consequences, prison life, future plan are summarized to give a clear picture about the study. The poor family background, poverty, broken homes, illegal relationship, marital maladjustment, conflict prone relationship are the causes. The childhood criminal record of the individual and their family members/relatives has a considerable impact for their present position. Reform in the prison life and future rejuvenation programmes are essential to light lamp in the lives of those fallen women. The suggestion is claimed under two headings. The first one for preventive programme, where in community, development programmes, police, justice system, Government agency, mass media, correctional social work, NGO's have an important role to play. In the second heading—suggestion for welfare and rehabilitative programmes covering prison facilities–medical and psychiatric, health services, effective individual counselling, education, vocational training, guidance are the aspects covered. The role of Social workers is very much emphasized follow of study is on another area suggest it which required wider planning and training by social scientist, social workers, and which creates need for future research.

Acknowledgement

There are so many who have helped hand in hand to ship this boat safe shore. Not as a formality but as a duty We sincerely acknowledge the Guide Dr. M. Lakshmana Singh, Professor and Head, Dept. of Sociology, Bharathiar University, Coimbatore, under whose constant encouragement and supervision this work has been completed.

Bureau of Police Research & Development is greatly obliged for their financial support throughout the research.The various prison officials of both Vellore and Madurai Mr. Rajkumar, Mrs. Narmadhabai, Mrs. Rajasundari are remembered for their continued support and cooperation during the field visits.

We sincerely express our gratitude to the Management and Faculty belonging to Social Sciences and Social Work of both Arul Anandar College (Autonomous), Madurai and Sacred Heart College (Autonomous), Tirupattur, North Arcot District.

We also greatly indebted to the inmates of both the women prisons in Tamil Nadu for their excellent cooperation and patience in responding to our queries without much hesitation. We also believe that this work could definitely bring some relief and rehabilitation in their life.

Our kind remembrance are due to Ms. Rama Lakshmi and Mr. Balamurugan of Professional Computers, Thirunagar,

Madurai for their preparation of manuscript with utmost care.

We take the privilege in thanking our family members for their encouragement and support without which this work would not have been possible.

We are with sincere gratitude thankful to Shri Kripal D. Joshi, Production Manager, Anmol Publications Private Limited, New Delhi for his kind cooperation and taking much pain in bringing out this book at his earliest.

Finally we acknowledge our heartfelt thanks to those who read this material and offer suggestion so as to encourage us to probe further into the field.

Authors

1
Introduction

There is hardly any society which is not beset with the problem of crime. It is a grave social problem faced by every society. Crime may be considered as an omission of an act which the law of the land expects the individual to do or commission of an act which it forbids to do. In the legal terms Crime may be defined as 'any form of conduct which is declared to be socially harmful in a state and as such forbidden by law under pain of some punishment' (Bhattacharyya, 1992). In other words crime is intentional act or commission in violation of criminal law committed without defence or justification and sanctioned by the law as violation or misdemeanour.

It is an unpalatable truth that crime is not only a fact of life but a way of life as well, since the bulk of human behaviour described as 'criminal' has been accepted as rationalized by many on grounds of expediency, necessity and compulsion. Hence it is understood that crime is an act forbidden by the law of the land and for which penalty is prescribed. The law of the land varies from place to place.

An act considered criminal in one place may not be the same in another place. It is Barnes and Tecter (1944) who gave a definition for crime in the following words, "Crime is a form of antisocial behaviour that has violated public sanction to such an extent as to be forbidden by the statute". So crime is more of a legal term as it is mostly explained in terms of law.

Crime is the major phenomenon of modern civilized and advanced society. It is a known fact that the available statistics on crime covers only those arrested and convicted, or the crime known to the police and judiciary and even these figures are not reliable.

It is argued by most of the social scientists that crime is the problem of the youth, since the persons involved in criminal activities mostly belong to the age group of 20-30 years. It is observed that there is a rapid rise in the relative frequency of criminal acts through the ten years and a peak is observed at around the age of 20 years.

The topic of women and crime has recently developed into a broad field of research in the field of Social Work, Sociology, Criminology and Law. For centuries, the criminal behaviour of women has been a neglected area of research. The special problem of the delinquent women were neglected at all times (Smith, 1965), through world-wide statistics on the incidence of crime exhibit a general increases in the rate of female criminality in many countries. It is since the last decade that the social scientists and criminologists have shown an inquistness towards women. Inspite of the strategic position of women in all societies and varying notions regarding their involvement in crime, there are only limited number of empirical research and do not yet have a comprehensive data on this social issue (Shukla and Saxena, 1984; Joseph, 1992; Saxena, 1994).

Though male criminality is still far greater than female criminality (Rani, 1979), the number of criminal offences committed by females has increased at a much higher rate than the number of crimes committed by males. The rate of crime is steadily increasing day by day all over the world India being no exception.

In India it is estimated that the female crime rate has increased by 362.53% for a period from 1971 to 1990; but for male it is only 146.70% (*Indian Express,* dated 12th November, 1992). Socially the crimes committed by the females are considered to be more serious when compared to the male criminality, because of the pivotal role played by a woman as wife, mother and caretaker in the family is salient significant. Hence the female criminality is considered more dysfunctional than male criminality.

There are various studies conducted on women criminals in abroad (Pollak, 1950; Wolfgang, 1958; Gluck, 1960; Smith, 1962; West, 1965; W.T. Thomas, 1967; Cowie, 1968; Creesey, 1971; Adler, 1975; Datesman, *et.al.* 1975; Smart, 1976; Price, 1977; Fox and Hartnegal, 1979; Austin, 1980; Campbell, 1984; Heidensohn, 1985; Gelstrope, 1986; Naffine, 1987; Edwards, 1987; Abbot and Wallace, 1990; Harris, 1993) and in India (Ahuja, 1970; Rani, 1980, 1981, 1987; Singh, 1981; Bhanot and Misra 1978; Sharma, 1965; Shastri, 1975; Sivanandam, 1974; Sohani, 1975, 1989, Rao, Sanyal, Agarwal, Ramadevi, Mohan and Singh all in 1982; Trivedi and Krishna, 1983; Ghosh, 1986; Nagla, 1991; Joseph, 1992; Saxena, 1994) as well.

One of the early women researches in India, Raj Kumari Sharma has done research on women criminality (1963) in Uttar Pradesh. A systematic presentation in book form on '*Female Offenders in India*' was done by Ahuja (1969). Various research projects on women criminality, sponsored by agencies like Bureau of Police Research and Development, Ministry of Social Defence, National Institute of Criminology etc., have created much interest on the subject and have been made to understand the socio-economic conditions, causes, consequences, nature and pattern of women crime in India (Ahuja, 1969, 1970), (Bhanot and Misra, 1978), (Nagla, 1982, 1991), (Rani, 1980, 1981, 1987), (Sivanandam, 1974), (Sohani, 1975), (Singh, 1981, 1983), (Trivedi, 1983), (Saxena, 1994).

On the sociological perspectives on women criminals, studies conducted by Ahuja (1969, 1970), Nagla (1982, 1991), Rani (1980), Joseph (1992) and Saxena (1994) are important. On the Psychological perspectives studies of Sanyal (1981) and Sharma (1963, 1987) are noteworthy. On the Criminological perspectives various researches are available in India. Studies like *Women Prisoners in Tamilnadu* (Prasad, S.K.K. 1981), *Women Murderers in Tamilnadu* (Prasad and Krishna, 1982) and *Female Criminality: Causes and Consequences* (Ramadevi, 1982) were conducted on criminological perspectives.

In India female criminality is prominent among the young women. It was observed from various studies (Rani, 1982, 1987; Nagla, 1982, 1991; Joseph, 1992; Saxena, 1994) all over the country that the women criminals were in between the age group of 20 to 30 years. They are not mentally and physically matured enough (since their age at marriage is very low) to cope with the role expected of them from their husbands and in-laws. They mostly belong to low social and economic status in the society. Their monthly income is also low.

With regard to the geographical background female crime is reported more from urban areas than rural areas. Illiteracy is reported to be an important factor in female criminality. All these studies show that the criminality of women is on the increase and claims serious consideration. Today women akin to men are taking part in all types of criminal activities involving physical prowess and the use of strong weapons (Rani, 1977). The changing role, shift in occupation and status, the concept of women emancipation, economic independence and political independence open the gate way for women to engage in various activities and hence the exposure to criminal activities is more that in the past.

Nowadays women in wide varieties of crime like Murder, Theft, Adultery, Kidnapping, Blackmailing, Smuggling, Shop lifting, Larceny, Dacoity, Illicit distillation, Drug trafficking and Prostitution. The pattern of crime varies from place to place and time to time. It is noted from the official statistic that women crimes are higher in states like Tamilnadu, Andhra Pradesh, Assam, Kerala, Maharastra, West Bengal, Himachal Pradesh and Jammu & Kasmir.

Tamil Nadu is the 11th largest state in India and occupies 4 per cent of the country's total area. It ranks fourth in the country in the incidency of crime and is one of the five states which recorded highest number of theft cases during 1981 (Sivamurthy, 1987). All India data on crime indicates that criminally among women was the highest in Tamil Nadu (8,306) followed by other states (*Crime in India,* 1983 : 70) and hence occupying the first place in women criminals rate.

Considering the world women criminal population, women in India are less criminal at least to the official records. As far as women crime is concerned they are under represented considering their proportion in the total population (Srivastava, 1984). It was observed from 1971-1978 over eight years, that the female crime has increased by 55.90 per cent as against the male crime which increased only by 41.87 per cent. Considering increase in crime as per thousand persons, female crime has increased by 50 per cent while the increases in male crime recorded only 30.58 per cent (Singh, 1971). Significant percentage of female criminals come under the heads of kidnapping and abduction, robbery, dacoity, fraudulent offences and offences of miscellaneous type.

The crime by women are committed in single or in accomplishment with others. In crime like illicit distillation, gambling, prostitution and dacoity female seek the help of the men folk to accomplish their 'Profession' easier. With regard to murder, mostly the victims are persons known to them already or often their own relatives. In most cases, it is observed that women criminals seek the help of kin members as their 'accomplice' in committing crimes. (Rani, 1982, Nagla, 1991).

It may be said that the female crime is the resultant factors of human needs such as, biological, social, economic and psychological needs, human nature such as her adjustment with husband, family and society and the environment which are accountable for developing the criminal tendency among women.

There are various reasons found to be responsible for the women criminality. These are broadly classified into Social, Economical, Psychological and Biological. Lack of education, competition, conflict, social disorganisation and mobility are the factors classified under social causes. The economic causes include desire for more and quick wealth, extravagance, industrialization and urbanization.

Under the psychological causes, emotional instability neurosis and psychosis are listed. Under the biological causes insanity, hormonal changes, defective glandular or nervous system and physical disability are attributed. There are specific reasons like selfishness, disobedience, stupidity, impoliteness, quarrelsome nature, arrogance, narrow mindedness, suspicious nature and illegitimate relations are also found contribution to female crime.

A study conducted in India found the following factors as conflicting areas for female criminals. They are husbands having the habit of drinking, gambling, prostitution and drug addiction, lack of interest in family life, forced marriage, illegal contact of the females, jealously due to the husbands illegal relationship, low income and excessive expenditure, conflict over sex and conflict over property (Prasad, 1982).

Pre-menstrual period is a stressful period for women. It was observed that 61.6 per cent murders were committed by women during this stressful period (Singh and Singh, 1979). During this period the hormonal changes induce women to engage in criminal activities or during this period women are liable to be detected for this criminal conduct. Pre-menstrual period is accompanied with irritability, lethargy, depressive and water retention and these symptoms make women to behave impatient, violent and emotional (Patel, 1974). Pre-menstrual tension was present among 50 per cent of the 95 prisoners (Singh and Singh, 1979).

The crime done by women draws much attention and is seriously looked into than the male crime, because of their pivotal role and the central figure in the family. Their participation in criminal activities leads to continuous deterioration. When a crime is committed by a female it has its repercussions on herself, husband, children, family, relatives, neighbours and on the society at large. For the individuals fall of status, social disgrace, stigma and stress; for the husband his familial role and sexual life; for the children, their social and economical development; for the family its role and functions; for the relatives and neighbours their interpersonal relationships and for the society, its very organisation. The stigma of having been in the prison has much more adverse consequences for women than men (Srivastava, 1994).

Prisons are generally set up to safeguard the safety and foster the rehabilitation of the criminals. With a view to fulfil this twin objectives, certain basic pre-requisites like orientation, classification, education, vocational training, work programmes, health, recreation and counselling are furnished to all the prisoners.

Apart from the basic amenities welfare services are also provided in the prison and there is a separate Welfare officer to look after the services. The welfare programmes comprise of

- Recording the case histories of prisoners on admission.
- Identifying their socio-economic problems.
- Corresponding for settling their property, land, matrimonial and familial disputes and
- Arranging recreational and educational programmes.

Women prisoners, as Dhar (1983) opined are no doubt worried about their family, particularly children, yet the foremost thought which exits in their minds at all times is what the future has in store for them. Women prisoners find it difficult to set back into the folds of the family members after release. Most of them therefore remain in perturbed about the dark future clouds and really do not know on whom to bank upon. The prison adjustment of women criminals reflected in abundance the symptom of hopelessness, uncertainty and anxiety, almost all of them think that their fate is sealed (Srivastava, 1984).

Rehabilitation process starts from the prison and ends when a criminal is settled again in the society after release. Rehabilitation is the process in which the criminal must experience, as if attained, more socially acceptable life on return to society. The various programmes like social case work, community link services, educational programmes, vocational training, recreational services and after care services are adopted to rehabilitation programmes follow up or after release programmes should be given due emphasis for the successful rehabilitation; since the very motto of rehabilitation programme lies in making such women acceptable.

Need for the Study

The present study has significant role to play in controlling the criminal behaviour among women and to find out ways and means to rehabilitate those who have already entered into the criminal system. At this juncture an evaluation of the functioning of women prisons is also important.

The criminality of women has been a neglected field of research due to the fact that their number is very small. There is a definite need for more indepth and intensive study on female criminality to acquire greater insight into the problem. For the past two decades the topic of women and crime has begun to draw much attention because of the recent interest in women and their development.

It is also a fact that the concentration of women offenders was highest in the State of Tamil Nadu (*Crime in India*, 1983 : 70). Female crime rate is growing at a steady pace in Tamil Nadu (*Compendium of Crime and Police Statistics of Tamil Nadu*, 1988). The Indian look at the women criminals has not yet adequately dealt with and has much to be done in the treatment and rehabilitation. The lack of purposeful and perspective analysis of issues concerning women, crime and the criminal justice system hinders our way in understanding, treating and rehabilitating the women criminals. The fact of our key interest in the subject may be attributed to the pervasiveness of the belief that the problem of the women criminality has not yet assumed any alarming dimension warranting focused attention, action or research (Srivastava, 1984). Hardly very few empirical studies are available on Social Work perspectives.

From Social work perspective, understanding of female offender is vital for designing of policies and programmes related to them. Added to this, the thought and knowledge towards women criminals were also meager. Hence an attempt is made to conduct an ellaborate empirical study on Social Work perspectives on women criminals with special emphasis to family of orientation, family of procreation, details about husband, measuring of consequences on individual, children, family and society at large, prison facilities available, future plan after release and suggestions for rehabilitation.

Objectives Of The Study

The following are the objectives of the present study:

- To understand the socio-economic background of female criminals.
- To know the particulars regarding family of orientation.
- To trace the details of family of procreation.
- To know the cause, nature and pattern of crime among women.
- To measure the consequences of female criminality on individual, children, family and society at large.
- To assess the facilities provided in prison and the impact on prison life.
- To study the future plan of the respondents and perceived acceptance of family and society and suggest suitable preventive and rehabilitative programmes.

Methodology

The study on 'Women criminals in Tamil Nadu' is of explorative in nature. It explores the socio-economic conditions, nature and pattern of crime, causes and consequences on individual, children, family and society, particulars of family of orientations and procreation, details of husband, facilities available in prison and their future plans after release.

Universe and Sampling Frame

There are two prisons exclusively meant for women and managed by women in Tamil Nadu. One is situated in Vellore in North Arcot Ambedkar District and the other in Madurai, Madurai District. The special prison for women in Vellore was started on 15th April 1930. Since than it was administered by the Superintendent, central prisons. Vellore (meant for males) upto 1965. After that a separate lady Superintendent has been appointed. The authorised accommodation of this prison is 412. The convicted prisoners from various districts like Madras, Chengelpattu, North Arcot Ambedkar. Thiruvannamalai Sambuvarayar, Dharmapuri, Salem, Erode Periyar, Coimbatore, and the Nilgiris are housed here.

Recreational facilities and cultural programmes are organised to enlighten the prisoners. It has a hospital with a strength of 20 beds and one Civil Assistant Surgeon has been appointed to look after the health needs of the inmates. Adult education, creche, children who are living along with the prisoners. A separate unit to manufacture cotton tapes and twisted thread which fetch earning to the inmates. The prison personnel includes a Lady Superintendent, a Lady Welfare Officer, a Lady Matron, a Lady Civil Assistant Surgeon and other clerical and security staffs.

The women prison in Madurai was bifurcated from Vellore women prison on 1st July 1987. It has the capacity to accommodate 200 prisoners. The convicted prisoners from various Districts like Trichy, Dindigul, Madurai, Virudunagar, Ramnad, Sivagangai, Trinelveli and Kanyakumari are housed in this prison. It has no hospital facility of its own. A separate Medical Officer has been appointed to look after the health needs of the prisoners.

There is no Vocational training or work in the prison available at present. One Lady Dy. Superintendent, a Lady Matron, a Lady Medical Officer and other necessary clerical staff and security staff have been appointed to administer the prison.

Inmates in both these prison constitute the 'Universe'. From the statistical data obtained from the prison department, Tamil Nadu, it is observed that both convicted and under trial prisoners are housed in these prisons.

The 'convicts' are those who are awarded imprisonment by the court of law for their criminal conduct and undergoing imprisonment during the time of study in the women prisons.

The 'Under trial prisoners' are those who are housed in such prisons and for them the trial is pending before the court of law.

Sampling Frame

There is fluctuation in the number of prisoners housed in these prisons. Before selecting samples average number of intimates per day was calculated taking into account the records of 30 days. For the purpose of calculation, records from Vellore and Madurai prisons were separately treated. In each place convicts and the under trial prisoners formed sub-units. From the data it is observed that the average number of convicts in Vellore is 39 and it ranged from 35 to 43; and in Madurai the average is 58 and it ranged from 51 to 68. Hence all the convicted prisoners during the study period were selected for detailed study. Thus a sample of 94 convicted criminals was obtained.

In the cases of under trial prisoners the average worked out to 42 and 20 for Vellore and Madurai prisons respectively. The actual ranged from 20 to 47 in Vellore and from 17 to 39 in Madurai prison. In keeping with the time and resources constraint it was decided to select 50 per cent of the under trial prisoners from the average.

In Vellore prison, in one particular day the under trial prisoner's record was obtained from the prison and listed then all the odd numbers were picked up and the interview only two or three respondence a day some of those who were listed as samples left the prison and the new pool of under trial prisoners came in. Then the new under trial prisoners were listed and the odd numbers were picked up. By this way 21 under trial prisoners were interviewed in Vellore prison.

The same procedure was followed in Madurai prison to select Under trial prisoners. The list was prepared and all the even numbers were picked up. There are 10 respondents and all the even numbers were picked up. Thus the sample contained 94 convicted criminals (38 + 56) and 31 Under trial prisoners (21 + 10). They were interviewed in detail.

TABLE 1.1

Representation of Sample in Both Women Prisons

Type of Inmates	*Prisons*		*Total*
	Vellore Prison	*Madurai Prison*	
Convicts	38	56	94
Under trials	21	10	31
Total	**59**	**66**	**125**

Tools of Data Collection

A structured Interview Schedule was constructed to collect data from women criminals. It consists of Personal profile, Particulars of family of procreation, School history, Parental treatment, Residential description, Childhood criminal behaviour, Details of husband, Employment details of the respondent, Enquiry for murderers, Enquiry for non-murderers, Particulars of juvenile and adult crime record, Causes, Consequences on individual, children, family and society with a five point scale, Prison life, Satisfaction level of prison facilities available with a five point scale, Suggestions by the respondents to improve prison life and Future Plan after release.

Period of Study

The study was conducted during September 1992 to March 1993 in Vellore and Madurai women prisons in Tamil Nadu. Data were personally collected by the researcher using interview schedule. It took 4 to 5 hours to complete one schedule. The data were collected during the months of September 1992 to March 1993. Personal observation, discussion with the prison personnel and police officials and criminal records in the prison also form the part of data collection.

Techniques of Data Collection

The following two techniques were used for data collection. They are Personal observation and Interview. Though observation methods various information were collected while being present in the prison. Number of units paid to the prison enabled the researcher to understand the prison and its function. During the course of the interview close observation was possible to gather information regarding behaviour of the inmates, their inter-personal relationships with the staff and inmates, etc. During the administration the interview schedule the researcher opted more for an informal rather than a formal interview.

It was more or less like a discussion rather than questioning them. This technique was very much helpful to establish a rapport with them which enhanced the purpose much easier. The respondents were very well participated in the discussion and revealed information freely without any hesitation though the researcher was a male.

Operational Definitions

Women Criminals—A Women who has been found guilty of criminal behaviour convicted under Indian Penal Codes and sentenced to imprisonment. The Under trial prisoners were also considered as prisoners for the purpose of the study.

Crime Involving Murder and Non-murder—Under the murder type crimes like murder, dowry murder, attempted murder, attempted suicide are classified. The non-murder type consists of crime like theft, kidnapping, smuggling, quarreling, crime relating to drug, illicit distillation and prostitution.

Crime Relating to Victim and No-victim—Under the crime involving victim, crimes like murder, activities like attempt to murder, hurt, kidnapping and quarreling are included. Crimes like theft, smuggling, drug trafficking. Illicit distillation and prostitution are listed crimes not involving victim type.

Crimes Relating to Person, Property and Morality—Under the crime against person crimes relating to murder, kidnapping and quarreling are included. The crime against property and other crimes includes theft, smuggling gold, smuggling sandal wood, illicit distillation, drug related crimes and borrowing stolen property (henceforth called as crime against property). Under the crime against morality, prostitution is included.

Long-term Prisoners and Short-term Prisoners—Long-term prisoners are those who are punished for a period of 10 years or more and the short-term prisoners are those whose terms of imprisonment is less than 10 years. The under trials are considered as prisoners for the purpose of the study.

Convicts and Under Trials—Convicts are those who are legally identified as criminals and undergoing punishment during the study period in the women prisons of Tamil Nadu. The Under trials are those who are housed in such prisons and for them the trial is pending before the court of law.

Chapterization

The present study has been chapterized into nine.

The first chapter deals with Introduction and Methodology. In the Introductory part, the scope and importance of the study and objectives of the study are dealt with. The Methodology consists of research design, universe and sampling frame, tools of data collection, techniques of data collection, period of study and description about Vellore and Madurai women prison where the samples were taken.

In the second chapter the review of literature pertaining to women criminals are discussed and due emphasis is given to nature and pattern of crime, causes and consequences, trends in crime rate, prison life, welfare services provided, rehabilitation programmes and various studies conducted in India and abroad are presented with statistical data.

Personal profile of the women criminals such as age, education, marital status, occupation, income, caste, religion and domicile are analysed in details and compared with nature of crime committed for further understanding in the third chapter.

The fourth chapter deals with the details of family of orientation comprising of the family background, the household income, educational level of the family, parental treatment and residential description.

Fifth chapter explores the details regarding family of procreation such as household income, educational level of the family, size of the family, marriage particulars of the respondents and husbands, and illtreatment, if any, faced by the respondent.

Childhood criminal behaviour, nature and pattern of crime, causes, details regarding murderer and non-murderer, age at crime done, distribution of the study sample in various districts of Tamil Nadu and arrest particulars are analysed in the sixth chapter.

In the seventh chapter the consequences felt and/or experienced by the respondents due to the Criminal Act on individual, family, children and society were measured and analysed.

Chapter eight deals with the prison life in general, welfare facilities provided in the prison and respondents satisfaction level towards it, impact of prison life and rehabilitation programmes, future plan and the perceived problems they would face after release.

The summary, conclusion and suggestions made are presented in the ninth chapter.

Limitations of the Study

The study attempts to find out the socio-economic background of the females who have been prisoned in Tamil Nadu women prison during the course of the study. Both convicts and under trials were considered as respondents in the present study. This is purely a socio-eco-culture approach to understand the problem of female crime in social work perspective.

At geographical level the study is confined to Tamil Nadu state. In the present study no attempt has been made to test any hypothesis or validity of any criminological theories.

2
Review of Literature

The women and has recently been attracted much attention due to the fact that the crime rate among women is on increase. There are various factors found to be responsible for that. The problem of women and crime is so serious that the consequences of women on the social structure is greater as women performs the role of mothers, wife, householder and caretaker. To identity the nature, extend, pattern and consequences of these women with a view to prevent as well as rehabilitate one who entered into the system; probe into the basic issues pertaining to women and crime are crucially needed. To better our understanding it is essential to analyse what is crime, theories specially meant for women criminality. Various studies conducted in India and abroad, statistics available on women criminality, causes, factors attributed to the increasing crime among women, prison life, facilities and rehabilitation programmes available for them. As a first step, in the following paragraphs meaning of crime, theories involved in crime are dealt with so as to have a basic understanding.

What is Crime?

In any society people have some norms, belief, customs and traditions which are implicitly accepted by its members and conducive to their well being and healthy all-Round Development Infringement of those cherished norms and customs is condemned as anti-social or criminal. Hence crime may be considered as immoral, sinful, antisocial and unethical behaviour. The crime may be defined as 'an act which a particular social group regards as sufficiently menacing to its fundamental interests, to justify formal reaction to restrain the violater' (Bhattacharyya, 1992).

The Italian School of Criminological thought formulated that the crime is an act which affects the basic moral sentiments of piety and probity. Similar to this definition Stephen (1960), has defined crime as an "act which is both forbidden by law and revolting to the moral sentiments of the society."

Emile Durkheim (1951) contented that 'crime is a normal phenomenon of every society' and he further explained that 'any society is composed of persons with angelic qualities and would not be free from violations of the norms of that society'. In fact, crime is a constant phenomenon changing with the social change.

Various Theories on Crime

There are number of divergent theories advanced by various social scientists for explaining the phenomenon of crime. The researchers from various disciplines such as social work, sociology, biology, psychology, geography, criminology and law have explained crime in their own way.

In Biological theories the scientists like Baccaria (1870), Jeremy Bentham (1925), Lomboroso (1911) and Glucks (1950) have contributed much to be biological theories in explaining the criminal behaviour. These theories explain the criminal behaviour in terms of the glands, body structure and low intelligence and only under the most favourable conditions can such individuals avoid criminality. But in the later years the validity of this school of thought was questioned and the concept has changed from biological to social and environment.

The psychological theories explain that the individual is disposed towards crime on account of certain personality traits as different from the social environment. The dynamic psychologists argued that the psychopathic personality and neurotic personality patterns emerge out of the differential development of id-ego-superego structure of the individual. The contributes to this school of thought like Sigmund Freud (1919), Jenkins (1944), Erickson (1950), Tappen (1960) and Blumberg (1974) are worth mentioning.

In sociological theories the phenomena of crime cannot be explained without reference to the mores, laws, customs and traditions, —the agencies of social control. When an imbalance is created between the cultural goals and the institutional means then the resultant factor is the development of criminal attitude. Crime is the outcome of the disparity between what people are trying to expect and what are really made available to them. (Cloward and Ohlin, 1960).

The Economic theories of crime contended that criminal behaviour is the resultant factor of the economic needs arising out of poverty, unemployment, low income, high cost of living, high expenditure etc. The various scientists like Bentham (1825), Voltaire (1960), Rouseeu (1960), Walsh (1930), Healy (1936) and Paranjappe (1975) contributed to the economic theories of crime. But it is widely accepted that economic factors alone are not responsible for the development of criminal attitude.

The political theories of crime however explain that the criminal law is being used by those in power to maintain their control over others (Quinney, 1975). The contributions made by Wright (1970), Turk (1972) and Venugopal Rao (1980) added weight to these theories of thought.

HISTORICAL PERSPECTIVES OF WOMEN CRIMINALITY

The criminality of women has been gaining much attention only in the recent past since their participation in the criminal activities has increased at a much higher rate. To have an understanding the historical perspectives of the issue is crucial importance.

Quetelet (1835) was the first scientist in the nineteenth century to inquire into the female criminality. In 1919, Lomboroso attributed certain physical characteristics to deviant women.

In the beginning of the 20th century, the concept has changed from physical characteristics to social and economic factors in understanding the women criminality.

Women Criminals

The criminality of women has long been a neglected subject of research. Criminology has been a traditionally male endeavour with the male scientists studying predominantly male offenders (Gelsthrope, 1986). It has been reminded that men overwhelmingly dominate in number, those who legislate our laws, those who relay and interpret these events for us in the media (Price, 1977). Perhaps due to their relatively small number, their predominately non-militant posture and the apparent infrequency of over brutality by their keepers, women prisoners have been neglected (Haft, 1980).

It has been the traditional opinion of criminologists and social scientist that women commit relatively few crimes and that when they do so they some how betray their womenhood by venturing out into a reserve of man. In the last decade the proportion of female arrests among the total number of persons arrested increased rapidly. This seems to be an indicator of the increasing deviance among the women.

In the recent past women have been participating in various aspects of social life including academic, scientific, culture and other productive and non-productive activities. The growing participation of female in these fields may be one contributing factor for the increase in the crime rates among women.

Major Theories of Female Criminality

There are various theories formulated by the social scientists for explaining the causation of women criminality. The main theories are Strain theory, Learning theory, Masculinity theory, Control theory, Labelling theory and Women's Liberation thesis.

Strain theory emphasises that the crime is caused by pressure, strain or tension , when frustrations occurred while facing obstacles to their achievement, the individuals behave definitely in order to release their tension or to action their goals through illegitimate means (Merton, 1949; Durkheim, 1951).

Learning theory focused upon the fact criminality is a learned behaviour. A persons associations with criminal persons and ideas have great role to play in developing, criminal tendency. Sutherland Ant Crssey's (1966) differential association theory is based on this idea. It states that a person will become criminal if he or she associates more with criminal than with anti-criminal people and ideas. The contributions of Glaser (1956) and Burgess and Akers (1966) are note worthy. This theory suffers with many setbacks by offering an empirically vague concept and a tautological explanation.

Crime is learned behaviour. Naffine (1987) identified nine factors which involved in the learning of criminal behaviour.

Masculinity theory is based on the idea that the criminal activities warrant masculine characteristics to execute. The criminal—darling, toughness, aggression, use of physical force, fast movements, etc., are necessary elements involved mostly in criminal activities.

Control theory argues that when the social control is locking the tendency to behave defiantly is more, in other words lack of control causes crime. The control theorists like Walter Rockless (1973), Ivan Nye (1958) and Hirschi (1969) have contributed to the subject by explaining the casual factor of conformity as containment, social control and bond.

Labelling theory was formulated with concept that when people are labelled as 'criminals' by their super ordinates it produces an unfavourable consequences for the individual so labelled. The social scientists like Howard Beoker (1963), Harria (1977) and Fox (1977) contributed much knowledge to this theory.

Under the Women's Liberation thesis it is stressed that in the modern times women have started participating in liberation movements. The liberation movement has brought out more masculine characteristics in women such as assertiveness, aggressiveness, competition and toughness. In addition the concept of liberation has opened structural opportunities to engage women in criminal activities.

There are also various theories formulated by different scholars Sutherland (1970), Cohen (1955) and W.I. Thomas (1967), available in understanding the female criminality on the biological and psychological perspectives. Later other theories advocated by scholars like Cloward and Ohlin (1960), Deming (1971), Alder (1975), Simon (1976), Quinney (1977) and Steffensmier (1978) stressed the need for considering the environmental stimuli in understanding the criminality of women.

Applicability of Male Criminal Theories to Females

Since earlier times the theories formulated for explaining the criminal behaviour the criminal behaviour are based on the 'male' model since the subjects studied are males and also the ones who conducted such studies were composed of male dominated population. Hence attempts were made to fit these theories to females. Adler (1975) and Simon (1975) have conducted research in these lines. In an another study conducted by Datesman, Scarpitti and Stephenson (1975) the utility of traditional theories of deviances in explaining women criminality was done. A detailed research on the same line was conducted by Simons, Miller and Aigner at the end of 1976 in Iowa State.

Nature of Women Crime

Women are engaged in wide variety of crimes. Unlike in the past women actively participate in all sorts of crime as men do. They are not only confined to particular types of crime which does not involve toughness of aggression, but they also engage in various other types of crime which warrants 'maleness'.

Women engage in wide varieties of crimes like murder, theft, adultery, kidnapping, blackmailing, smuggling, illicit distillation and prostitution. Some of the women criminals capitalize their charm and feminity entrap the man usually involves a large sum of money.

Kawale (1982) found that the crimes committed by women are pick pocketing, dacoity with arms, theft and forcible theft. They belong to such group or communities where they operate equally with men to commit crimes mostly involving force and trickery. The women seek the help of men folk in committing crimes like illicit distillation, gambling, prostitution and dacoity.

In many places women criminals plays a passive role in the game and leaves it to her male companion to bear the punishment. It is a fact that large number of crimes for which men are convicted were really inspired by women. Many married women due to their over expenditure and self indulgence induce their husbands to resort to dishonest means to keep them supplied of money. The women criminals in such cases play a role of the aider or abettor in crime.

With regard to the place selected by women to commit crimes, Wolfgang (1958) observed that most of the homicides committed by women took place with in home and kitchen. As far as murder is concerned the place for committing crime is either in bed room, kitchen or in the backyard of the house (Rani, 1983). And the Victim is mostly the person living closer to them (Pollak, 1950; Smith, 1962; Smart, 1976; Wolfgang, 1958; West, 1962; Ahuja, 1970 and Rani, 1983).

The crime pattern among women varies from place to place and time to time. Female crime is higher in the states of Andhra Pradesh, Assam, Kerala, Maharashtra, West Bengal, Himachal Pradesh and Jammu and Kashmir. The increase in some of the states can be partly explained by the growing participation of women in the economic activities of the states and a perceptible bid for greater equality in economic roles (Nagla, 1991). The official statistics released by various agencies indicate that significant percentage of females involvement had been under the heads of kidnapping and abduction robbery, dacoity, fraudulent offences and offences of miscellaneous type. It is strange to note that women had also been arrested under Arms Act. Opium Act, Explosive and Substances Act, Prevention of Corruption Act and other miscellaneous Acts.

New Trend in the Nature of Women Criminals

Women criminals involving in crimes like dacoity, robbery, theft, kidnapping and abduction, pick pocketing, chain or watch snatching, cheating counterfeiting and drug trafficking are nowadays operating with crime syndicates in bigger cities and towns. Srivastava (1984) revealed that the decent looking women smugglers and call-girls trained in tricks and masking their deceit and deception under the cloak of a respectable is a new phenomenon in bigger cities and metropolises. But it is true that these women belong to the lower social and economic class whose services are hired by by such 'organisations' meant for this purpose.

Females are now being found not only robbing banks single handedly, but also committing assorted armed robberies, muggings, loan-shirking operations exertion, murders and a wide variety of other aggressive, violence-oriented crimes which previously involved only men (Adler, and cultural-today women criminal differs from their predecessors not only in attitude and aspirations but in basic intelligence (Price, 1977). A high rate of property offenders may engage in robbery one day, burglary the next motor theft the day after. On the whole it is quite clear that these women should be treated different from the traditional criminals. These women who have been in the headlines as murders, bank robbers, kidnappers, hijackers and revolutionaries were considered as anew bread of female criminal more violent than the traditional female offenders (Shukla and Saxena, 1984). On the whole it is quite that these women should be treated different from traditional criminals.

It has been found that there is relatively high proportion of women among persons arrested for embezzlement and fraud, forgery and counterfeiting, larceny and theft while prostitution commercialised vice, are through to be behind the scenes the managers (Johnson, 1966). It is firmly believed that female crime is coming to resemble more closely that of man probably as a result of increase in employment opportunities of women (Simon, 1975). It has also been claimed that compared to women in the past, females today tend to commit more Masculine crimes (Adler, 1975; Gibbons, 1977); more violent crimes (Adler, 1975; Bruck, 1975): more Serious crimes (Simon, 1975; Datesman *et al,* 1980): more Male dominated crimes (Inclardi and Slegel, 1977) and more White collar or occupational crimes (Simon, 1975, Widom, 1978).

Empirical Studies in India

Recent trend of interest has been found in the area of women and development among the educational planners and policy makers. Hence women from the general topic for discussion and research. There has been a small group of writing specifically concerned with women and crime in India. The important among them are Ahuja (1969,1970) Bhanot and Misra (1978).

Sharma (1965), Shastri (1975), Sivanandam (1974), Sohani (1975), Singh (1981), Rani (1980, 1981, 1983, 1987), Nagla (1982), Rao (1982), Prasad (1982), Sanyal and Agarwal (1982), Ramadevi (1982), Mohan and Singh (1982), Trivedi and Krishna (1983), Ghosh (1986), Sohani (1989), Joseph (1992), Saxena (1994) etc.

Profile of Women Criminals Observed in Various Studies

It has been observed from various studies conducted that women criminals mostly belong to the age group of 20 to 40 years. (Ahuja, 1969, 1983; Nagla, 1991; Joseph, 1992; Saxena, 1994) hence it may be considered as the problem of the youth. This age group suggests that women below 20 years are physically and psychologically immature and they are supposedly less capable of committing serious crimes owing to their minimal involvement in social and economic affairs of family life in India (Srivastava, 1984).

Most of the women criminals are illiterates. Only a statistically insignificant fraction of the women criminals are literates with educational standards upto primary or middle class. When the women criminality increases the educational level decreases and *vice versa.* The correlation between education and women criminals was found high but negative (-80) (Gautam, 1982), Contrary to this, recent trends show that more number of educated women were participating in criminal activities (Rani, 1981).

An overwhelming majority of women offenders are married, deserted and divorced, with married ones being the highest in the whole lot. Since most of them are married they are not in a position either physiologically or socially to fulfil the expections of the husband and in-laws, resulting in conflicts between them and ultimately lead them to engage in criminals activities. The married ones who entered into criminal system are persons who had undergone a very stressful relations with their husbands. Their marital life had been riddled with severe conflicting situations involving oppression. Cruelty, rejection and humiliation.

It was observed that the crime is low in low castes (Ahuja, 1969), but in another study it was evident that a slightly more than 50 per cent women criminals belong to backward castes. On the whole the incidence of crime is high in low economic class (Kawale, 1982).

More than three fourth of the female criminals belong to Hindu religion. The proportion of women from Muslim, Sikh and Christian religions is less than their actual proportion in the total population.

While calculating the monthly income of the women criminals it was observed from various studies that more than 50 per cent of them belong to the income group ranges from Rs. 100 to Rs. 150. A high percentage of women offenders belong to economically disadvantage class with total family income being hardly adequate to make both ends meet (Srivastava, 1984). In another study more than 90 per cent of the women criminals came from Rs. 50 to Rs. 200 income group (Prasad, 1982). A study conducted by (Rani 1981) in Andhra Pradesh State revealed that the per capita income is less than two hundred rupees per month. A greater proportion i.e. 92.5 per cent was living with a per month. Taking into consideration the average per capita income of Andhra Pradesh state (Rs. 83.3 per month). 92.5 per cent of the belong to below the average state per capita income. Further, 81.7 per cent of them live below poverty line (Rani, 1981). Some women of this low economic class kill their husbands because of man's addiction to costly and wasteful vices like heavy drinking, drug addiction, prostitution and gambling (Srivastava, 1984).

Most of the women criminals belong to the low cadre of occupations. They are not gainfully employed and work as essentially housewives, maid servants, menial jobs and casual labourers.

It is surprising to note that majority of women criminals belong to urban areas while nearly eight per cent of the country's total population lives in rural areas. Most of the studies supported this observation (Ahuja, 1969; Rani, 1983). This suggests that women criminality in India is not an entirely rural phenomenon as popularly believed (Srivastava, 1984). In urban areas these women criminals are the residents of hut and slum colonies. It is obvious that the urban areas have more illegitimate structure than the rural. With the regard to the nature of crime, women living in urban areas were involved mostly in moral offences followed by property offences, smuggling and rioting and in rural areas the women were involved predominantly in offences against person and excise offences (Rani, 1981).

Family Background

Family is the basic unit of the society where the learning, personality, character molding and other needs of the individuals are properly looked into. When the family is not in a position to cater to these needs to its members then the deterioration takes place and which may lead the members then the deterioration takes place and which may lead the members present in the family is inter-dependent and most significant (William, 1993).

When the relations are not cordial it leads to continuous deterioration and many a time make the member to indulge in criminal activities. Ahuja in his study (1970) observed that stressful family situation conflict prone relationship with-in-laws compel women to involve in crime and commit heinous crimes like murder.

In the family of orientation stressful situations due to parental conflicts, extravagance of parents, bad habits of parents and siblings, illicit relationships of family members and quarrel-some nature of parents have its own influence on the behaviour of the women. In the family of procreation, various factors like maritial maladjustment, imbalance in sex related matters, non adjustment of the husband and in-laws, infective role performances on the part of the female and the maltreatment of the family members in the family of the procreation have been identified as the reasons for the females involving in criminal activities. Broken home factor is one of the most important causes often quoted while explaining women criminality. It was observed that women like men are also motivated to do crime (Paramaguru, 1984), Adwani (1978) contended that the main reason is due to immaturity to perform maritial roles and activities to shoulder the family role expectations which consequently lead husband and in-laws to maltreat women which may in turn lead females to behave deviantly.

A study conducted in Tamil Nadu by Prasad (1982) revealed that husbands bad habits of drinking, gambling, drug addiction, husbands nature being argumentative, suspicious bad temperament, aggressive, greedy and his illicit relationship with other women are the major area faced by women murderers. In another study conducted by Rani (1983), it was observed that domestic factors like deprivation of love and care of their parents or husbands and in-laws or a combination or both victim provocation and lovers of friends instigation were contributory factors in women crime. Domestic quarrels, maritial maladjustments were the main motives behind homicides (Trivedi and Krishna, 1983).

Victims/Clients

The term 'Victims' and 'clients' are used depends upon the crime. With regard to the crimes like immoral offences, excise offences and smuggling the term 'client' is used in the sense that any one of who pays get the required service by approaching the practising deviants. In fact the 'victim' are really the clients and are bit 'victimised' in any normal sense of the term. With the regard to the crimes against property etc., the term 'victim' is more appropriate. Under the crime against person head, the victim mostly belong to the close associates of women criminals. The victims belong to husbands family, close relatives, co-partners in property and persons known to them.

Acceptance of Crime

It is one of the problems often faced by the researches in the field of female criminality that the statements given by the imprisoned women and the versions of the court are entirely ore partially different. Some of the convicts did not agree with the nature and degree of involvement in crime as recommended in the court judgement. These differences must also kept in mind while understanding the women criminals. In the study conducted by Rani in Andhra Pradesh during 1974-1978, among the 120 samples studies 27 (22.50%) respondents have done crime and in 11 (9.16%) cases there was a partial agreement or disagreement. These limitations must be kept in mind while doing analysis and understanding the women criminals. Since to achieve the task of bring out the truth at every stage of the study is a difficult work. In a study conducted by Ahuja of female offenders in 1969 in Rajasthan, among the 49 samples studies only 24 (48.98%) female prisoners have accepted that they have done the crime and the other equal percentage of 51.02 did not accept their crime.

Accomplice

Whenever physical strength is required, women seem to be taking assistance of others, males or females with whom they have intimate or kindship. It is revealed that the women criminals seek the assistance of their lovers or friends or family members or other kinsmen at different phases of their offences (Rani, 1981). The crime were committed either main role or the subsidiary role. They belong to such communities where they operated equally with men to commit crimes mostly involving force and trickery.

Crime Rate in United States

The crime rate among women has increased sharply in recent years. Arrests of women have increased by two-third in less than a decade. Between 1978 and 1983 arrests of women for 'serious crimes' ranging from auto-thefts to murder went upto 52 per cent; the increase for men in this period was only 8 per cent. Not only the arrest rates increases but also the convicted and prisoners rate increases (Price, 1977). In United States it was observed that the arrest rates for serious crimes increased by 18 per cent for male and female the increase by 62 per cent between 1960-65. The percentage increases of women criminals between 1962 to 1965 was four times than it had been observed during the earlier years (Sabharwal, 1982). The eight years data of a male and female arrests under the IPC crimes was analysed by Singh (1981). She took 1971 to 1978 years data for her analysis. Over eight year the female crime has increased to 55.90 per cent as against the male crime which has increased only to 41.87 per cent, considering 1971 being the base year.

The crime figures in United States of America for a period from 1960 to 1978 showed a dramatic increase. Based on the UCR Report in 1979 the arrest rates have nearly tripled. The largest increases are found to be for larceny (arrests have risen from 32.34/100.00 in 1960 to 230.39 in 1978) and for fraud and embezzlement (from 8.29 to 102.36/100.00). Large arrests have also occurred in arrests for forgery (the rate has increased fivefold); and armed robbery and receiving/possessing stolen property.

Crime Trend in India and Tamil Nadu

In India the crime rates are apparently deceptive. For 2.5 per cent (198%) of the criminal population numerically reported a substantial number (52,059), among whom 1298 are homicidal offenders and 7269 are property offenders (Statistics for a single year—Crime in India, 1983). The recently available national data further indicate that criminally among female is highest in Tamil Nadu (8306) followed by Maharashtra (8112) and lowest in Nagaland (Nil) among the States (Sohani, 1989).

In Tamil Nadu criminal statistics indicate a slow but perceptible increase in female crime for the last decade, indicating that while offender constitute 3.5 per cent of the total population in 1978, they constitute 6.3 per cent in 1988 (refer table number 2 in appendix).

Female participation is notably increasing in property crimes (theft, burglary, robbery) followed by murder. Through these are greater number of women reported for both riots and miscellaneous offences, these are generally characterised by non-serious offences (refer table number 3 in appendix).

Variations in number of persons arrested by sex interms of index with references to base year 1971. The female criminals constitute 3 to 6 per cent of the total criminal population in terms of percentage. Female crime indicates a clear galloping increase as opposed to male rates which are maintaining a slow and steady pace of growth. In absolute number the rate of female crime is negligible but in relation to percentage of growth this appears as a notable group in Tamil Nadu (refer table number 4 in appendix).

Reasons for Low Arrest and Crime Rates among Women

The authorities in the criminals system are very reluctant to arrest, prosecute and convict female criminals because of their 'femaleness' (Rao, 1981). As far as crime is concerned the women crime statistics are under reported considering their proportion to the total population in comparison with male. The masked nature of the women criminals and factors of chivalrism and paternalism has its influence on the police and judiciary.

Added to this Pollak (1950) contended that the female crime rates are under estimated due to the fact that many of the crime done by women are under reported. The following are such crimes: (a) thefts by female servants, (b) thefts by prostitutes, (c) blackmail, (d) sex offences, (e) homicides and (f) infanticides.

There are various reasons found to be responsible for the low rate of arrest and crime rates among women. The factors involved in the lower arrest rate and for the apparently lower female participation in crime are listed by Haskell and Yablonsky (1978). They are:

- Females roles are more clearly defined.
- Females are more closely supervised.
- Females receive greater protection.
- Females have opportunity for household employment.
- Male roles are more active.
- Men are likely to be chivalrous.

- The public perceives men and women differently.
- The police react differently to men and women.

The police and the judiciary have been thought unwilling to apply a criminal label to the 'fair sex' which is, as a consequence under represented in the criminals statistics (Adles, 1975; Price, 1972). The same view was expressed by Scutt and Jocelynne (1979) that in the area of crime the authorities are reluctant to arrest, prosecute and convict women criminals because of their 'femaleness'. Thus it is imperative that when such crimes are reported the crime rate will increase significantly.

Rao (1981) opined that low criminality among women can be ascribed to the general treatment available to women in the criminals justice system itself. In India women are less criminal atleast to the official figures. As far as crime is concerned their proportion to the total population (Srivastava, 1984). But it is doubtful that to what extent that these statistics are reliable is an unanswered question.

Causes of Women Crime

There are various reasons found to be responsible for the criminality among them. These causes may be classified under various heads like biological, social, economical, psychological, personal and familial. In some cases it is very difficult to identify a particular criminal activity. Sometimes a specific factor in a particular situation becomes the causes for a specific type of criminal behaviour. Hence in the analysis of causation the possibility for different kinds of interpretations has to kept in mind and one has to carefully discern the real case of causes for a given criminal behaviour (Rani, 1981).

Economical Causes

Financial constraints have been on the important direct contributory causes for the acts of theft. In a country like India this factor hardly needs any detailed explanation. In fact financial factors are the chief factors which give rise to different situations of stress and strain compelling the individuals to think of and take to different types of deviant behaviour.

Social Factors

The various social factors such as bad influence, employer's ill-treatment, environmental influence, feeling of betrayal and initiation into criminal activities plays an important role in the women criminality. Located as they are in poor conditions, women are exposed to a variety of undesirable practices and behavioural patterns and they slowly imbibe the same behavioural patterns from the surrounding and take to all sorts of deviant behaviour in the footsteps of their reference groups or individuals (Rani, 1981). It is also revealed that the deviant kith, kin and close relatives have their own influences on the women criminals.

Sexual Relation or Conjugal Family Life

In most of the cases of women criminals it was observed by various studies that these women had experience dissatisfied sexual/conjugal relations in their life. They or husbands also accounted for illegal contact with other persons. Expect in cases such as those of excise offences and smuggling, in a majority of the other offences unhappy conjugal relationship and/or illicit sexual relations became prominent at one stage or the other (Rani, 1981).

Women Status

Studies were conducted to examine the status of women and the involvement of criminal activities. There is a close association between the economic position of the women and her involvement in crime was observed. A study conducted by Cathy (1990) on the status and women criminality in comparison with male made the following findings; (1) The more unfavourable women's economic condition relative to males greater the proportionate female involvement in crime condition relative to males greater the proportionate female involvement in crime relative to male involvement; (2) The greater the opportunity for traditional female consumer oriented crime the larger the proportionate involvement of females in offending than male; and (3) The higher the level of formalization of social control when the official rates of female crime than male.

Changing Social Roles of Women

The lower social status and the underprivileged position of women in the Indian society have certainly contributed to the liberal provisions relating to the arrest, bail and custody of women criminals (Nagla, 1991). Crime may even be a rational and coherent response to women awareness of the social disabilities imposed on them by class and gender roles (Abbot and Wallace, 1960). The increase in the incidence of female criminality is attributed by some to the increase in the status of women (Giallombardo, 1976). The role of wife, lover or girl-friend is important of a woman. Now the pattern of the role-behaviour is changing, so also the pattern of crime among women (Nagla, 1991).

As women's traditional activities in society change and diversity, she has many more opportunities to break the law (Fox and Hartnagel, 1979). Simon (1975) concluded that women's participation in selected crimes will increase as their employment opportunities expand and as their interests, desires and definitions of self shift from a more traditional to a more liberated view. In a study conducted in Canada by John Fox and Timothy F. Hartnagel (1979), observed that if female labour force participation rate increases substantially in future years it is possible that this variable may come to have a greater effect on female conviction rate. Women's role outside the home provides them with more opportunities for committing crime especially those of white collar crime (Baunach, 1977). Finally it is concluded that chages in various aspects of women's structural position in society affect female crime rate. Exposure to criminal risk increases due to decreased guardianship either because people live alone or with unrelated persons or because labour force participation removes both husbands and wives from their households during working hours (Cohen and Land, 1990).

Psychological Causes

Sanyal and Agarwal (1982) found that out of a total 69 female convicts 73.91 per cent are found with high feeling of insecurity and 81.61 per cent are with negative self-esteem. These negative self-esteem is found more in the lower social and economical strata of the convicts.

Pre-Menstural Period

It is considered that pre-menstrual period is the period of stress and strain to women. The pre-menstrual tension is accompanied by irritability, lethargy, depression and water retention and these symptoms make women more ill tempered, impatient, violent and emotionally deranged (Patel, 1974). It was revealed in a study conducted by Singh (1980) that about 53 per cent of the criminals committed their crimes at the time of their pre-menstrual period. It was found that 61.6 per cent of the murders were committed during the pre-menstrual (Singh and Singh, 1979). It was also statistically observed that crime and menstruation are statically correlated (Horney, 1981).

Environmental Factors

It was Ahuja (1969) who made research to look into the situation and environmental variables compelling women to commit crime. Stressful situations, maladjustments, disharmonious maritial relations, conflict-prone relationships with husbands and in-laws and maladjustments in interpersonal relationships with in the family are causes found to be responsible for women criminality. Rani (1983) in her study observed that in slightly more than 70 per cent cases domestic factors played an important role indisposing of women to entertain attitudes of victims, provocation, lover's/ friend's instigation played a major direct role in pulling out such criminal proneness. The pathological family backgrounds like broken homes, parental rejection, faulty discipline by parents, undesirable peer group relations and socio-economic conditions play a major role in the crime among women (Eswari *et al.*, 1982). The causes of women criminality were largely due to broken homes and crises of changing social values (Misra and Gautam, 1982). Rani (1983) analysed in her study that women were deprived of love of their parents, or other elders negation of their attitude to divorces or desert their husbands and various other unhappy incidents in their life lead them frustrated and behave deviantly.

Substantial amount of evidence over the years suggest that sex roles and the position of women have not undergone much change in the recent years, especially in the direction that would lead to change in the women crime (Nagla, 1982).

Violent crimes like murder and culpable homicide not amounting murder, the factors mostly held responsible are family quarrel, desire for revenge and retaliation to redress the situation of continued repression, humiliation and rejection, sexual incompatibility, husbands illicit sexual contact, the desire to flee from the clutches of a tyrannical husbands, mother-in-law and the women's attempt to more out of the maritial bonds in order to live an emotionally and sexually satisfying life (Srivastava, 1984). Once a woman experience harsh behaviour from her husband and his kith and kin and an unfriendly domestic atmosphere, she makes every possible effort to escape the situation by taking resort to illicit contacts outside wedlock or by taking to different kinds of deviant behaviour not excluding prostitution. In case of the unmarried, predominantly broken homes and/or bad associations with males and females led them to deviant behaviour (Glueck, see in Cowie, Cowie and Slater, 1971; Punekar and Kamala Rao, 1962; Ram Ahuja, 1969; Rani, 1981).

Impact of Urbanization and Modernization

It is assumed that the problem of women criminality emanates from the rapid transformations of the society from past tradition to modernity (Misra and Gautam, 1982). The conflicts created between the cultural goals and institutional means available to achieve them lead to aggression resulting in deviance among women (Cohen, 1970). This contention is also well supported by the empirical findings in India (Rani, 1983).

Urbanization has lead to the breaking up of joint families. The rising prices have forced women to seek jobs in urban as well as rural areas. The exposure to the world of work naturally brings about a desire for franchise. But when the Indian women seeks freedom at home and asserts for rights, it creates further streets. The male supremacy which is challenged thus, naturally wants to re-establish itself and there are resultant, stresses, strains, jealousies in the marital relationship, resulting in frictions, conflicts, even oppression of the female which ultimately she unshackles through murder. Apart from the stresses coming from the husband front, there are also the in-laws who further make the miseries by claiming dowry and in the absence or shortage of which they start penalizing the daughter-in-law. This adds to the marital maladjustment of the female (Nagla, 1991).

Consequences

The consequence of women criminals are more complicated in nature and leads to continuous deterioration

Crime done by women are dysfunctional than the male crimes because women are having greater consequences on the society than man. Socially crimes committed by females are compared to be more serious to the male crimes since the vital role played by the women as mother, wife and more to say a central figure in every society. Hence the role makes the female crimes more dysfunctional. When a crime is committed by a female it affects the individual, children, husband, family and the society at large. The consequences on the family is at large since it influences the children and their development; the husband his familial role and sexual life and to the neighbours and friends their interpersonal relationships. Reuben (1949) pointed out that a crisis is created in the family by the committing of crime by a women and consequently her imprisonment. This crisis requires a new type of adjustment on the part of all the members of the family.

During such crisis somebody has to perform role of the mother, householder, cook, caretaker which were being done by the imprisonment women. To say more specifically on the part of the husband some sexual adjustment is also required. It also results in closing of ranks, shifting of responsibilities and activities of the office to another women containing the necessary family routine, day to day work, maintaining husband-wife relationship by correspondence and visits and utilising the resources of friends, relatives and neighbours.

Women Prisons

Prison earlier times meant just for the custody of the prisoners. In earlier days when the female criminals were in smaller number they were housed along with male criminals in separate enclosures. Imprisonment not only prevent the individual to commit for a specific period but also make them isolated from others so that others would not commit crime on them out of vengeance. But due to rapid rise in the number of women criminals separate women prisons were established in order to stop overcrowding and also to prevent any untoward incident in the prison. These institutions have all the facilities, etc. The criminals arrested under Immoral Traffic Act and Sexual offences were housed separately.

According to the statistics given by the All India Committee on Jail Reforms (1980-83) there are 76 central jails, 280 district jails, 822 sub-jails in the country. Out of these 1995 jails, there are only 4 separate jails for women prisoners throughout the country, one each in the states of Andhra Pradesh, Maharastra, Tamil Nadu and Uttar Pradesh. In Tamil Nadu one more prison meant for women was established in Madurai in 1987. There are two jails for women, one each in Bihar and Rajasthan, but they form part of the central jails where men are also confined.

Today prison life is seen something more than a matter of walls and bars of cells and locks (Ghosh, 1986). The prison is a community within the community. It is a social system which despite occasional disruption, function reasonably well (Cloward, 1960). Srivastava (1977) has concluded in his study that prison as a system may develop a sub-rosa organisation and may maintain all those institutional characteristics which form an essential part of any social organisation. In such a social system a prison is once again able to maintain a status and role in the prison community.

The All India Committee on Jail Reforms (1980-83) made several observations regarding the conditions of women prisons. They are as follows:

- Only small section of the men's prisoners is generally provided for confinement of women prisoners where all categories of them are handled together in the same wards and barracks.
- Women prisoners whether in sub-jails, district prisons, or central prisons in most states have to walk through

men's section and sometimes have to go through men's section and often have to go through experiences which are humiliating.

- While living conditions, treatment and training for male prisoners are nowhere near the desired level, the lot of women prisoners is much worse. Women in prisons suffer from unhealthy living conditions, exploitation, unnecessarily prolonged severance from their families and lack of gainful and purposeful employment.
- Women continue to be in jails for long periods sometimes for very minor violation of law, unable to defend themselves and totally ignorant of ways and means of securing legal aid or help even to write a petition for quick disposal of their cases. They are not aware of the rules of remission or premature release and live a life of resignation at the mercy of officials who seldom have understanding of their problems.
- The kind of shy, inhibited village women that usually land jails have no courage to communicate their needs to the male staff posted in their jails. They have no means of communicating their needs to the higher officials as there is hardly any woman officer at the headquarters of the prison departments who would appreciate their needs and requirements.
- Women prisoners confined in separate enclosures, the keys of which are held by male staff, are far from safe from moral danger. They are exploited and given little opportunity to express their grievances.

They cannot even express their grievances to visitors. Thus visitor never get know the truth. Women prisoners also do not complain of the realities because of the fear of consequences which they have to face.

Women Prisons in Tamil Nadu

There are two prisons exclusively meant for women and managed by women in Tamil Nadu. One is situated in Vellore in North Arcot Ambedkar District and the other in Madurai, Madurai District. The Special prison for women in Vellore was started on 15th April 1930. Since that it was administrated by the Superintendent. Central Prisons, Vellore (meant for males) upto 1965. After that a separate lady Superintendent has been appointed. The authorised accommodation of this prison is 412. The convicted prisoners from various district like Madras, Chengelpattu, North Arcot Ambedkar, Tiruvannamalai Sanbuvarayar, Dharmapuri, Salem, Erode, Periyar, Coimbatore and the Nilgris are housed here. Recreational facilities and cultural programmes are organised to enlight the prisoners. It has a hospital with a strength of 20 beds and one Civil Assistant Surgeon has been appointed to look after the health needs of the inmates. Adult education, creche, children education are the other extended facilities to the inmates and their children who are living along with the prisoners.

A separate unit to manufacture cotton tapes and twisted thread which fetch earning to the inmates. The prison personnel includes one lady Superintendent, one Lady Welfare officer, and Lady Matron one Lady Civil Assistant Surgeon and other clerical and security staffs.

Facilities available in Vellore Prison

The prison are supplied with throw ball, tennis and other games articles and allowed to play during holidays. A cultural committee is functioning in this prison and arrangements were made to organise cinema, drama, dances and other cultural programmes.During festival times students from nearby institutions were contacted to entertain the prisoners. There is a 35 mm projector is available to screen the feature films.

Television and Radio are available to recreate the inmates. Religious and moral lectures were arranged to strengthen the ethics of the prisoners. On October 2nd prisoners welfare day has been celebrated. There were also various other facilities like free legal aid, library facility, availability of news papers and magazines and canteen facilities available to meet the needs of the prisoners. Sanitation and water facilities are looked into with great concern.

The women prison, Madurai was bifurcated from Vellore Women Prison on 1st July 1987. It has the capacity to house 200 prisoners. The convicted prisoners from various Districts like Trichy, Dindigul Anna, Madurai, Kamaraj (Virudhunagar) Ramnad, Sivagangai, Tirunelveli and Kanyakumari are housed in this prison. It has no hospital facility of its own. A separate Medical Officer has been appointed to look after the health needs of the prisoners. There are no vocational training or work in the prison is at present available. One Lady Dy. Superintendent, one Lady Medical Officer and other necessary clerical staff and security staff have been appointed to administer the prison.

The nutritious diet scheme has been implemented in these prison partly. As a first step Pongal, Uppuma and Rice Kanji are being issued for the morning break-fast. The prisoners are at present given meals for midday and evening, consisting of rice, dhall, vegetables, greens and butter-milk. Expectant mothers and feeding mothers are given special diet as per medical recommendation.

Rehabilitation of Women Criminals

Rehabilitation is the medical term. In medical sense, rehabilitation means the restoration of the handicapped individuals to the fullest physical, mental, social and economic usefulness of which they are capable, including ordinary treatment in special rehabilitation has been borrowed from the medical field to the social scientists to provide orientation and due to the emergence of the concept of 'Welfare State'.

In social sense, rehabilitation means the process or technique of re-educating and redirecting the attitudes and motivations of a delinquent criminal or a social deviate so as to bring his/her own willing acceptance of social regulations and legal restriction (Fairchild, 1964). According to Jarvis (1978) rehabilitation is the resocialization process which an offender must experience if a more socially acceptable life is to be attained on return to society. Rehabilitation of women is a complex and difficult task. As far as the women involve in moral offences the task of rehabilitation is much more difficult.

An Evaluation of Women Prison

There is strong reason to believe that the opportunities offered to the women are substantially inferior to those provided to their male counterparts in all areas of education, rehabilitation, occupational programmes, social and cultural programmes, employment opportunities and even medical care (Sikka, 1986). In almost all the prisons the women are treated with male model frame work programmes, which may not serve the purpose.

There are hardly six women prisons available in the country exclusively for women. All others are attached with the male prisons. The United Nations Standard Minimum Rules for the Treatment of prisoners recongnise the existence of institutions serving both men and women. The directions given is very clear that men and women shall, so far as possible be detained in separate institution, in an institution which receives both men and women the whole of the premises allocated to women shall be entirely separate.

With regard to the use of the prison labour in many women prisons of the women are idle 75 to 100 per cent of their working hours and they may "Sit" for months and sometimes years (Sikka, 1986). The data from various studies revealed that majority of the women in the prisons are married and hence most of them are mothers. Training in the areas of developing parenting skills, child care, nutrition, effective home management and counselling on marital relations are essentially required by these women criminals. Hardly little efforts have been taken in this regard.

As far as the medical care is concerned there are very few medical staffs available and periodical checkup is not done regularly. Medical care is the other aspect which must be under-scored (Sikka, 1986). The pregnant prisoners are given little attention during their prenatal and post-natal period.

The children along with the mothers in the women prison is an another area which needs considerable attention. Children of the offenders remain the hidden victims of woman's criminality, both inside the prison and outside. The facilities and treatment for such children are very low. In the words of Sohani (1978), Children in institutions often, unfortunately, are subject to the same kind of regimentation as their mothers are and it show. It is painful to see that happening to infants of two or three who, instead of being folded and played with, are made to sit in orderly rows with arms (for the benefit of visitors). There is no justifiable reason why institutional children's nurseries should be dreary places whereas those outside are designed to be cheerful and stimulation.

In many places women are housed within men prisoners who are living in jail within jail (Srivastava, 1984). Hence the opportunities enjoyed by male prisoners as a matter of rule may not be possible to their female counterparts. Added to this the women prisoners are engaged in manual and household occupations like cutting vegetables, cooking, tailoring, cleaning of grains and utensils, bakery and embroidery which makes them more of a household workers than self-sufficient.

Evaluation of Welface Services

First of all the training programmes conducted in various prisons are hardly server to the needs of the present day labour market. The trends are outdated and traditional ones. Trades like toy making, doll making, tailoring, garment manufacture, stitch craft, knitting, spinning, weaving, basket making, mat making, cooking, candle making, incense making, bangle making, flour and masala grinding, amber charkha and hidi and soap making. By means training the women prisoners can be effective household workers than the trades than to the individual needs of the prisoners. These so called 'rehabilitation programmes' (Srivastava, 1984). As Sohoni (1974) rightly evaluated that these training programmes are neither reflective of market labour requirement nor conductive to employment.

Secondly the trades are corporate in nature in such a way that the women prisoners cannot pursue any after release because of the large number of labour, capital and the problem of procurement of raw materials. Thirdly, the training in itself is inadequate. The skills taught cannot be compete with the skills available in the open market. Lastly, as Ansari (1982) pointed out that the procedure adopted for vocational training in prisons is on job training, the value of which is impaired by the fact that the jobs are overmanned and prisoners doing an assigned work, learn slow work habits which make them dull, docile and placid, doing them more harm than good.

Reasons for Ineffective Rehabilitation Programmes

It is an accepted fact that the rehabilitation programme is not successful in many cases due to various reasons. The very motto of the prison life lies on the rehabilitation programme. Failure in the rehabilitation programme is the failure in prison system itself. It is essential to find out the factors that hinders that successful rehabilitation programme. Some of them are:

- No definite aim of rehabilitation
- Degrading of inmates
- Not empirically verified
- Lack of public cooperation and support
- Feeling of neglect
- No systematic planning
- Lack of proper follow up programmes

On the evaluation of the rehabilitation programmes Srivastava (1984) has rightly pointed out that the rehabilitation and training programmes in women prisons are grossly ineffective. For reasons for such ineffectiveness he further contended that due to small proportion of women criminals it is rather difficult for the administrators and policy makers to innovate new methods of education and vocational training which could be of much use to the women criminals after release. Moreover the rehabilitation programmes have been administrated by males and also the prison system has been managed by men, primarily for men (Price, 1977). Hence the male model frame-work of rehabilitation programmes were tried to fit for the female.

In this context Srivastava (1982) outlined some of the essential requirements for a balanced rehabilitation programme which are given below.

Requirement for Effective Rehabilitation

- The underlying messages of institutional placement of such women and girls should be that they are being sent to specialized institutions for purposes of correction and rehabilitation and not for custody or confinement.

- The major emphasis in the correctional treatment afford to such women and girls in the institutions should be to create a desire for conscious guidance and the recognition of benefits in rehabilitation and the rehabilitation tools.
- The programme of behaviour thereby must exist and aid to rehabilitation therapy.
- Overcrowding in the institutions must be minimized as to make individualized treatment possible.
- To work programme of the inmates should be made interesting, profiting and economically rewarding for their future economic rehabilitation.
- The scientific procedure of classification should be strictly followed and the inmates more prone to correctional endeavours be kept away from those who are hard nuts to crack.
- The education should be planned in accordance with inmates personal needs and requirements.
- The correctional institution for such women and girls must become schools where inmates, through their close associations with the staff at every level can come to understand what it means to be a decent human being.
- Institutional incarceration should be sparingly used and that too for a microscopic minority the women and girls in moral and social danger who cannot be helped by other alternative services.
- The difficult transition to life in the world outside the gates protective institutions should be make smooth by a humans and efficient system of after care that may take over the responsibility and continue the effort till the ex-inmate is purposefully rehabilitate.

Role of Social Work in Criminal Settings

The motto of correctional settings is the social, economical and moral rehabilitation of the criminal. The training and the treatment given to the inmate should foster all-round development to the individual. Such a specialist function requires the cooperation and coordinations of the professionals like medicine, education, vocational, recreation, administration, security and social work. In probation and parole the scope of social work methods are preponderantly greater.

It is essential to understand the application of social work to the correctional settings in the light of the definition of social work seeks to enhance social functioning of individuals singly or in groups, by activities focussed upon their social relationship which constitute the interaction between man and his environment. These activities can be grouped into three functions: restoration of impaired capacity, provision of individuals and social resources and Social Group Work are the commonly employed methods in the criminal settings. A detailed explanation of these two methods are highly significant.

Social Case Work

The most important methods of social work which is predominately employed in correctional settings is social case work. It is defined as a method of social work which intervenes in the psychological aspects of a persons life to improve, restore, maintain or enhance his social functioning improve, restore, maintain or enhance his social functioning takes through a professional relationship between the worker and the person, and also between worker and the other individual whose intervention with the person affects his role performance. In this method an intimate close, face relationship is established with the social worker and the delinquents which can easily facilitate supportive guidance to the delinquents to solve his problem by himself. Normally there are three stages involved in social case work method. There are (i) case study (ii) diagnosis and (iii) treatment.

In the first step, the social case history of the client is to be collected by interviewing the client, her family members, friends, relatives and neighbours. Her socio-economic background, the environment where she lived etc., should be collected so as to have a overall picture of the client. The second stage comes with the diagnosis of the case by consulting with various experts in different fields in necessary in order to find out what is exactly her problem. In the third stage the treatment process starts. But it is to be understood that since from the beginning of the first stage, the treatment is started when the delinquent is interviewed by the social worker.

Short-term treatment programmes have been introduced to curb the inadequacy in social work programmes. Mangrum (1976) gave a proposal for short-term treatment used for programmes must aim at practical problem solving but not on character building or personality restructuring but on behaviour change through resolution of problems which give rise to illegal and/or antisocial conduct. The following steps may involve in the short-term treatment programme. Firstly the problem of the criminals should be identified and segmented in small components in such a way that he individually can handle easily. Although some of these problems will be internal and psychological, most will be external and environmental. In the next stage goals must be limited and reachable; limited achievements revolving round the specific problem areas and realistically attainable ends.

Social Group Work

Social Group Work can be defined as a process and method through which individual and groups in social agency settings are helped by a worker to relate themselves to other people and to experience growth an opportunities in accordance with their needs and capacities.

Group work is also one of the important methods of social work employed in correctional field. The objectives of group work is to help the individual for his personal growth, his adjustment to the group and society, recognisation of his principle that in every stage of life men in group. The family, school, association, peer group, club, communities, etc., are groups where one person has to live in one or the other. Hence the influence of the group on the individual and *vice versa* is crucial and significant (William, 1993). The role of the group worker is more of an enabler and he is link between the group and the agency.

He helps the group to determine its objectives purpose and goals to develop group feeling and consciousness, identity personal problems and help solve and individual to maintain relations with groups members in the words of Konpka (1956) the social group worker enables various types of groups to function in such a way that both group interaction and programme activity contribute to the growth of the individual and the achievement of the describe social goals. The objectives of the group work include provision for personal growth according to the individual capacity and need, the adjustments of the individual to order persons, to group and to society, the recognition by the individual of his own rights, limitations and abilities as well as his acceptance of the rights, abilities and differences of others.

Evaluation of Social Work Methods in Criminal Settings

The evaluation of social work methods in correctional settings should be paid due attention inorder to get feed back so as to improve the method. In a study conducted by Lipton, Martinson and Wilks (1975) after reviewing the empirical studies available in the field. They made the following recommendations. Social work has an improvement function to perform in combination with treatment and rehabilitation programmes. Moreover social workers must show innovate new ideas and methods of treating them. Lastly continuous evaluation must be done so as to rectify the mistakes and also should consider others reaction and feed backs to make the social work methods effective in criminal settings.

Additional Skills and Knowledge Required for a Social Worker

For an effective and successful correctional work the social worker must have the following additional knowledge and skills apart from his professional skills:

- Knowledge of delinquent and criminal behaviour.
- Knowledge of psychological and social strains which, in various constellations, press individuals towards such behaviour.
- Skills in identifying the social and psychological factors in the causation of particular delinquent criminal behaviour.
- Attitudes of acceptance of delinquent, and criminal deviant without condoning their anti-social behaviour.
- The readiness to work experimentally and without undue discouragement in the field where present knowledge is limited, prognosis is uncertain and failures frequent.

3

Personal Profile

It is very well known that the socio-cultural environment is correlated with crime rate. For any empirical study where human factor is involved the socio-cultural antecedents are given due emphasis and recognition.

To understand the crime as a phenomenon among women it is very much essential to probe into the personal and family profiles of the respondents. Such an analysis gains more importance in understanding and determining the social attitudes, behaviour and personality of the respondents. Hence in this chapter an analysis has been made to understand the age, education, maritial status, occupation, monthly income, caste, religion, domicile, particulars of family of orientation, family background, parental care and residential description. These socio-cultural antecedents are crossed with the type of crime done, for the purpose of comparative analysis.

As a first attempt personal profile of the respondents are taken into consideration.

Age

Research work done on female crime by various scholars have indicated that the involvement of young women (Ahuja, 1969: Adwani, 1978: Rani, 1981: Joseph, 1992) in criminal activities is more. Other studies (Saxena, 1994) revealed that

TABLE 3.1

Personal Profile

Variables	*Frequency*	*Percentage*
Age	**n : 125**	
Upto to 25 years	22	17.60
Mean	22.58	
S.D.	22.64	
26 to 30 years	32	25.60
Mean	28.19	
S.D.	01.64	
31 to 35 years	18	14.40
Mean	33.56	
S.D.	01.54	
36 to 40 years	16	12.80
Mean	38.00	
S.D.	01.59	
41 to 45 years	10	08.00
Mean	43.50	
S.D.	01.78	
Above 45 years	27	21.60
Mean	54.93	
S.D.	07.46	
Mean	36.24	
S.D.	12.05	
Years of Schooling (Education)	**n : 125**	
Illiterate	83	66.40
1 - 5 Years	11	08.80
6 - 8 Years	16	12.80
9 - 10 Years	10	08.80
11 Above	05	04.00

(Contd.)

Variables	*Frequency*	*Percentage*
Mean		02.03
S.D.		03.28
Occupation	**n : 125**	
Agriculturists	20	16.00
Trade/Business/Services	16	12.80
Traditional Occupations	14	11.20
Agri Coolie/Manual Work	49	39.20
Irregular/Unemployed	17	13.60
Illegal Activities	09	07.20
Marital Status	**n : 125**	
Married	63	50.40
Unmarried	05	04.00
Widow	39@	31.20
Separated	18	14.40
Caste	**n : 125**	
Schedule Caste	29	23.20
Most Backward Caste	33	26.40
Backward Caste	60	48.00
Forward Caste	03	02.40
Religion	**n : 125**	
Hindu	102	81.60
Muslim	008	06.40
Christian	015	12.00
Monthly Income	**n : 125**	
Upto Rs. 250	21	16.80
Mean	72.86	
S.D	102.38	
Rs. 251 to 500	26	20.80
Mean	401.48	

(Contd.)

Variables	*Frequency*	*Percentage*
S.D	065.67	
Rs. 501	26	20.80
Mean	669.23	
S.D	069.39	
Above Rs. 750	17	13.60
Mean	1376.47	
S.D	546.33	
Total	**125**	**100.00**
Mean	534.56	
S.D	434.80	
Residence Before Marriage	**n : 125**	
Rural	93	74.40
Urban	32	25.60
Total	**125**	**100.00**
Residence After Marriage	**n : 125**	
Rural	87	72.50
Urban	33	27.50
Total	**120**	**100.00**

* : not applicable to unmarried

@ : 7 respondents are widowed due to their act of killing their husbands.

middle aged persons were more in number. Hence in the present study an attempt has been made to find out the age distribution of the respondents.

It was found that the majority of the women criminals (70.40%) belong to the age group of below 40 years. A considerable to the age group of above 45 years. The men age of this age category (54.93) and the range (46 to 80) are notable ones.

The age of the respondents was observed as predicated and it supports the various studies conducted in this field in India. But the considerable proportion of above 45 years age group in the sampling suggests that the involvement of the middle age and old aged women in criminal activities is more and observed as a recent development.

Educational Status

Literacy and female crime rate are negatively correlated. When literacy rate decreases the crime rate increase and *vice versa* (Ahuja, 1969: 1991; Rani 1981). Educational institution have significant role to play in socializing the individual by inculcating the role and responsibilities in society. An analysis to this effect is followed to understand the educational status of the respondents.

The educational status reveals that 66.40 per cent of the respondents are illiterates and the remaining are literates. It supports the findings of various studies (Rani, 1983; Nagla, 1991; Joseph, 1992) and what is notable here is the increase in proportion of 'literate' women in criminal activities. It is inferred that the involvement of literate in committing crime is on the increase. The literate Population comprises of educated upto Primary School (11), Middle School (16), High School (10) and Higher school and above (5). Since majority of them were illiterates they cannot earn their livelihood and burden in the economic life led them to further stress and strain in the social life may be one of the determining factor for their criminal behaviour.

Marital Status

Studies revealed that married women tend to commit crime than unmarried, widowed and separated (Ahuja, 1969:

Saxena, 1994). Early marriage, not coping with the expectation of the husband and in-laws, lack of awareness on the new role and status in the family procreation and maladjustment play a vital role for the unmarried women to behave deviantly.

There was a more or less equal proportion of both married respondents and 'other' category. The 'other' category comprises of unmarried (4.00%), widow (31.20%) and separated (14.40%). It was contended that majority of the women criminals are married since the lack of adjustment involved in the family of procreation. Among the widow (39) those who are widowed due to their act was 7; (i.e. their husbands' were killed by the respondents).

Caste

Caste has its own influence on the individual since it is peculiar and traditional system in Indian society. To have an idea of the distribution of the respondents on the basis of their caste the foregoing analysis is made.

It is observed that nearly half of the respondents belong to the backward castes followed by one fourth of them belonging to the most backward castes. The scheduled caste population comprises a little less than one fourth of the total sample. A minimum percentage proportion is constituted by the forward caste respondents.

In this study the caste is classified into two broad categories namely. Low caste for the purpose of comparative analysis in the later part of the study. The Low caste include (i) Scheduled castes (ii) Scheduled tribes and (iii) Most backward castes and the high caste comprises of backward castes and forward castes. Both low caste and high caste share equal proportion of more or less 50 per cent each.

Religion

In Indian context, the role of religion is broadly classified into two types for the purpose of the study. They are Hindu and Non-Hindu including people from Muslim and Christian religions. The majority of the respondents (81.60%) belong to Hindu religion and the 6.40 per cent belong to Muslim and 12.00 per cent belong to Christian religion.

It is one of the reason that people continue to believe in primitive customs, habits and superstition, added with illiteracy and ignorance make them socially and economically weak and meek, and adding pressure ultimately responsible for the criminal tendency development.

Monthly Income

The level of income is an indicator to understand the economic position of the individual. It is a notion that low income group tend to involve easily in crime. Low paid jobs, poor economic conditions add pressure in executing her social economical role, individuals, 'habits and attitudes'.

Various studies revealed that the monthly income of the women criminals ranges from Rs. 100-200 (Rani, 1991; Ahuja, 1969). The income group has been classified into four categories for the purpose of the study. A good number of respondents (48.80%) belong to the income group of Rs. 251-500, followed by Rs. 501-750 category (20.80%), upto Rs. 250 category (16.80%) and above Rs. 750 category (13.60%).

The mean income of the respondents was calculated as Rs. 534.56 and the standard deviation is Rs. 434.80. It is interesting to note that the respondents income ranges from Rs. 250 to Rs. 3000. It is inferred that involvement of high income group in criminal activities is on the increase.

Residence—Before and after Marriage

It was observed in almost all the studies conducted in India that the female crime is relatively an urban phenomenon. Since most of the women criminals belong to urban rather than rural areas. But in this study it was found that three fourth of the women criminals belong to the rural areas (74.40%). The urban respondents comprises of 25.60 per cent. Hence it is inferred that female crime is not only an urban phenomenon as well.

When the residence after marriage was reported there was no significant difference found as far as their residence is concerned. It is also observed that the phenomenon of marriage took place from rural to rural than to rural to urban and *vice versa*.

Occupation

The occupation of the respondents revealed their economic status and position in the society. It is observed from the table that 3.1 per cent of the respondents engaged in manual work for daily wages in agricultural and other activities. There were also respondents who engaged in occupations like agriculture (16.00%), Trade, business and services (11.20%). It is also reported by the respondents that they engage in illegal activities (7.20%). It is also reported by the respondents that they engaged in illegal activities (7.20%) and justified it as an 'occupation'. The occupational status of the respondents were employed in low paid, irregular occupations. The low cadre occupations are understood along with their low economic conditions and poor standard of living.

Illiteracy, low cadre occupation with poor economic conditions make them more susceptible in crime. Moreover some of the respondents even considered their criminal activities such as prostitution, illicit distillation, smuggling, theft, etc., as 'occupation' or 'professions' traditional and menial occupations were the largest category where the respondents were predominantly distributed speaks of their low economic conditions, insecure occupation, inadequate working conditions. Added to this unemployment and lack of economic security are factors which influenced these women either directly to involve in criminal activities.

Details Regarding Respondents' Occupation

With a view to understand the relationship of work environment with crime committed the following analysis has been made. In various investigation done by scholars it was observed that women criminals were employed in low paid jobs. The lower paid occupation of the respondents indicates that their economic conditions is in distress. In order to balance the situation they indulge in criminal activities. Lower paid occupations are more closely associated with crimes relating to property and immorality.

Occupational Details

In order to know the relation between the occupation and work environment with the criminal behaviour of the respondents details regarding the occupation were analysed and presented in the table 3.2.

It is observed that only there were 92 respondents successfully employed in various occupations. Among them 77.17 per cent had not shifted their occupation and stuck on to that till they came to prison. Twenty one respondents (22.83%) had to shift their occupation due to illtreatment by the employer (9), less salary (7) and dissatisfied work environment.

It is inferred that illtreatment, less salary and dissatisfied work environment were contributing factors along with poor economic conditions, more conflicts and quarrels—in inculcating the deviant behaviour among the respondents.

Personal Profile with Nature of Crime

For the purpose of better understanding, the personal profile of the respondents are analysed in relation with the nature of crime done by them.

TABLE 3.2

Respondents Occupational Details

Item	*Frequency*	*Percentage*
Occupational Details		
Shifting of Occupation		
Shift in occupation	21	22.83
No Shift in occupation	71	77.17
Total	**92**	**100.00**
Shift in occupation	21	22.83
Reasons for occupational shift		
Illtreatment	09	42.86
Less salary	07	33.33
No satisfaction	05	23.81
Total	**21**	**100.00**

To facilitate the comparative analysis, the crime committed by the respondents have been classified into five sets of types. They are

(a) Crime related to murder and non-murder.

(b) Crime involving victim and no-victim.

(c) Crime against person, property and morality.

(d) Long-term prisoners and short-term prisoners and

(e) Convicts and Under trials.

(a) Crime Related to Murder and Non-Murder

Under the murder type crimes like murder, dowry murder, attempted murder, attempted suicide are classified. The non-murder type consists if crime like theft, kidnapping, smuggling, quarrelling, crimes relating to drug, illicit distillation and prostitution.

Out of the 125 respondents 56 (44.80%) belong to the murder type and 69 (55.20%) belong to the non-murder type.

(b) Crime Involving Victim and No-Victim

Under the crime involving victim, crimes like murder, activities like attempt to murder, hurting, kidnapping and quarrelling are included. Crimes like theft, smuggling, drug trafficking, illicit distillation and prostitution are listed under crimes not involving victim type.

Out of the 125 respondents 61(48.80%) belong to victim type and 64 (51.20%) belong to no-victim type.

(c) Crimes Relating to Person, Property and Morality

Under the crime against person crimes relating to murder, kidnapping and quarrelling are included. The crime against property and other crimes includes theft, smuggling gold, smuggling sandal wood, borrowing stolen property and also illicit distillation (henceforth called as crime against property). Under the crime against morality, prostitution is included.

The distribution of the respondents on crime against person, property and morality is estimated as 60 (48.00%), 45 (36.00%) and 20 (16.00%) respectively.

(d) Long-term Prisoners and Short-term Prisoners

Long term prisoners are those who are sentenced for a period of 10 years or more. The short-term prisoners are those whose terms of imprisonment is less than 10 years. The Under trials were also considered as prisoners for the purpose of the study. The long-term prisoners were 57(45.60%) and the short-term prisoners were 68 (54.40%) in the sample.

(e) Convicts and Under Trials

Convicts are those who are legally identified as criminals

and undergoing punishment during the study period in the women prisons of the Tamil Nadu. The Under trials are those who are housed in such prisons and for them the trial is pending before the court of law. The convicts constitute 94 (75.20%) and the Under trials constitute 31 (24.80%) in the sample.

For the purpose of comparative analysis the educational status has been classified into illiterates and literates; caste has been divided into low caste and high caste. Low caste comprises of schedules caste and most backward castes and the high caste comprises of backward castes and forward caste. The maritial status has been grouped into two as married and 'others'. The 'other' category includes unmarried, widowed and separated.

I. CRIME INVOLVING MURDER AND NON-MURDER

In table 3.3 the socio-cultural antecedents of the respondents are crossed with crimes relating to murder and non-murder.

Age

When the age of the respondents is seen along with the nature of crime committed by them, it is observed that, 32 respondents (25.60%) had committed their crimes at the age of 26 to 30 years; of this 15(46.88%) respondents had committed crimes relating to murder and the other 17(53.12%) have involved in non crimes. These respondents were followed by 27 respondents (21.60%) in the above 45 years age category, of which 17 (62.96%) of them have done murder related crimes and 10 (37.34%) had committed crimes of non-murder category. There were 22 respondents (17.60%) represented the under 25 years age category in which 7 (31.82%) of them were involved in murder related crimes and more than double the number of respondents (68.18%) committed crimes in the non-murder category, 18 respondents were seen. Out of this

TABLE 3.3

Crime Relating Murder and Non-Murder and Personal Profile

Variables	*Crime Relating to*		
	Murder	*Non Murder*	*Total*
1	**2**	***3***	***4***
Age			
Upto to 25 years	07 (31.82)	15 (68.18)	22 (100.00)
26 to 30 years	15 (46.88)	17 (53.12)	32 (100.00)
31 to 35 years	06 (33.33)	12 (66.67)	18 (100.00)
36 to 40 years	07 (43.75)	09 (56.25)	16 (100.00)
41 to 45 years	04 (40.00)	06 (60.00)	10 (100.00)
Above 45 years	17 (62.96)	10 (37.34)	27 (100.00)
Total	**56**	**69**	**125**
Education			
Literate	17 (40.48)	25 (59.52)	42 (100.00)
Illiterate	39 (46.99)	44 (53.01)	83 (100.00)
Total	**56**	**69**	**125**
Caste			
Low Caste (SC, ST & MBC)	26 (41.94)	36 (58.06)	62 (100.00)
High Caste (BC & FC)	30 (47.62)	33 (52.38)	63 (100.00)
Total	**56**	**69**	**125**

(Contd.)

1	**2**	**3**	**4**
Religion			
Hindu	47	55	102
	(46.08)	(53.92)	(100.00)
Non-Hindu	09	14	23
	(39.13)	(60.87)	(100.00)
Total	**56**	**69**	**125**
Monthly Income			
Upto Rs. 250	09	12	21
	(42.86)	(57.14)	(100.00)
Rs. 251 to Rs. 500	28	33	61
	(45.90)	(54.10)	(100.00)
Rs. 510 to Rs. 750	09	17	26
	(34.62)	(65.38)	(100.00)
Above Rs. 750	10	07	17
	(58.82)	(41.18)	(100.00)
Total	**56**	**69**	**125**
Residence Before Marriage			
Rural	50	43	93
	(53.76)	(46.24)	(100.00)
Urban	06	26	32
	(18.75)	(81.25)	(100.00)
Total	**56**	**69**	**125**
Residence After Marriage	**n : 54**	**n : 66**	**n : 120**
Rural	42	45	87
	(48.28)	(51.72)	(100.00)
Urban	12	21	32
	(36.36)	(63.64)	(100.00)
Total	**54**	**66**	**120@**

@ : Not applicable to unmarried.

N.B. : Figures within parentheses indicate percentage.

33.33 per cent were related with murder crimes and double the number 66.67 per cent represented who belonged to 36 to 40 age group, in which seven and nine of them committed crimes relating to murder and non-murder respectively. Finally, 10 respondents (8.06%) come in age group of 41 to 45 years, among them four have committed crimes relating to murder and the six others committed non-murder crimes.

It is concluded that except in the above 45 years age category in all other age categories the proportion of respondents belonging to non-murder crimes is higher than the respondents of murder related crime category. As far as the present study sample is concerned, it is inferred that higher proportion of aged respondents (above 45 years) found a predominant place in murder related crimes.

Education

Most of the respondents were uneducated, numbering 83 (66.40%) in the total sample of 125. Out of this 39(46.99%) had committed crimes relating to murder and 44 (53.01%) others had committed non-murder crimes. Among the literate population numbering 42(33.60%), 17(40.48%) had done crime of murder category and 25(59.52%) of them involved in non-murder crimes. There is no significant difference between the respondents of murder and non-murder related crimes as far as their education is concerned.

Marital Status

For the purpose of comparative analysis the marital status has been classified into two broad categories. One is married category and the respondents who belonged is unmarried, Widow and separated were classified in the 'others' category. There are 63 respondents (50.40%) in the married category. Among the respondents in the married category 39.68 per cent and 60.32 per cent belonged to murder and non-murder category respectively. In the 'others' category (62), there were equal proportion of the respondents (50.00%) belonging to both non-murder and murder related crimes.

Caste

For the purpose of the study the castes were broadly classified under two categories namely, low caste and high caste. Low caste represents the member from scheduled caste and most backward caste and the high caste comprises of background caste and forward caste respondents. More or less equal proportion of both low caste (62) and high caste (63) represented the study sample of 125. Among the low caste the proportion of respondents relating to murder crimes (47.62%) and non-murder crimes (52.38%). It is concluded that the proportion of low caste respondents was high in crimes relating to non-murder than murder.

Religion

Religious affiliation revealed than out of 102 Hindu respondents (81.60%), 47 were involved in murder related crimes and the rest (60.87%) have committed crimes relating to non-murder crimes. Among the non-Hindu respondents (23), 39.13 per cent involved in murder related crimes and the rest (60.87%) have committed crimes relating to non-murder category.

Monthly Income

Monthly income of the respondents brings forth the following details. There are 61 respondents (48.80%) who had a monthly income of Rs. 250-500; out of which 28(45.90%) have done crimes relating to murder and the rest of 33 (54.10%) committed crimes involving non-murder. Out of the 26 respondents (20/80%) who belong to the income category of Rs. 501-750, 34.62 per cent involved in murder related crimes and little less than double (65.38%) belong to non-murder category. In the Rs. 250 and below income category there were respondents (16.80%) in which 42.86 per cent and 57.14 per cent belonged to crimes relating to murder category respectively. Rest of them numbering 17(13.60%) were earning above Rs.750 per month in which 10 (58.82%) belong to murder related crimes category and other seven (41.18%) were in non-murder crime category. It is inferred involving in crimes relating to non-murder crime category. It is inferred that when the income level decreases the respondents involving in crime relating to non-murder increase and if the income increases murder related crime increases.

Residence—Before Marriage

When the residence of the respondents before marriage is taken into consideration, 93 respondents (74.40%) had lived in rural areas. Among the respondents who lived in rural areas (93), 53.76 per cent belong to the non-murder crime category. The urban respondents represented one fourth of the total population in the sample (32). Of this, highest proportion of 26 respondents (81.25%) committed relating to non-murder and the rest of 6 (18.75%) respondents committed crimes involving murder. It is inferred that the rural respondents tend to crime relating to murder rather than crimes relating to non-murder. For the urban respondents their proportion in crimes relating to non-murder is more than crimes relating to murder. Hence it is concluded that there is no difference in the above trend even after their marriage as far as their residence is concerned.

II. CRIME INVOLVING VICTIM AND NO-VICTIM

An attempt has been made to understand the personal profile of the respondents on the basis of crime involving victim and no-victim.

TABLE 3.4

Crime Involving Victim and No-Victim and Personal Profile

Variables	*Crime Relating to* Murder	Non-Murder	*Total*
1	*2*	*3*	*4*
Age			
Upto 25 years	08	14	22
	(36.36)	(63.67)	(100.00)
26 to 30 years	16	16	32
	(50.00)	(50.00)	(100.00)
31 to 35 years	08	10	18
	(44.44)	(55.56)	(100.00)
36 to 40 years	07	09	16
	(43.75)	(56.25)	(100.00)
41 to 45 years	04	06	10
	(40.00)	(60.00)	(100.00)
Above 45 years	18	09	27
	(66.67)	(33.33)	(100.00)
Total	**61**	**64**	**125**
Education			
Literate	19	23	42
	(45.24)	(54.76)	(100.00)
Illiterate	42	41	83
	(50.60)	(49.40)	(100.00)
Total	**61**	**64**	**125**
Age			
Upto 25 years	08	14	22
	(36.36)	(63.67)	(100.00)
Marital Status			
Married	28	35	63
	(44.44)	(55.56)	(100.00)

(Contd.)

1	2	3	4
Others (Unmarried, Widow and Separated)	33 (53.22)	29 (46.78)	62 (100.00)
Caste			
Low Caste (SC, ST & OBC)	29 (46.78)	33 (53.22)	62 (100.00)
High Caste (BC & FC)	32 (50.80)	31 (49.20)	63 (100.00)
Total	**56**	**69**	**125**
Religion			
Hindu	47 (46.08)	55 (53.92)	102 (100.00)
Non-Hindu	09 (39.13)	14 (60.87)	23 (100.00)
Total	**56**	**69**	**125**
Monthly Income			
Upto Rs. 250	09 (42.86)	12 (57.14)	21 (100.00)
Rs. 251 to Rs. 500	32 (46.08)	29 (53.92)	61 (100.00)
Upto 25 years	08 (36.36)	14 (63.67)	22 (100.00)
Rs.501 to Rs. 750	10 (34.62)	16 (65.38)	23 (100.00)
Above Rs. 750	10 (34.62)	07 (65.38)	17 (100.00)
Total	**61**	**64**	**125**
Residence Before Marriage			
Rural	53	40	93

(Contd.)

1	2	3	4
	(56.98)	(43.02)	(100.00)
Urban	08	24	32
	(25.00)	(75.00)	(100.00)
Total	**61**	**64**	**125**
Residence After Marriage			
Rural	43	44	87
	(48.28)	(51.72)	(100.00)
Urban	15	18	33
	(45.46)	(54.54)	(100.00)
Total	**58**	**62**	**120@**

@ : Not applicable to unmarried.
N.B. : Figures within parentheses indicate percentage.

Age

Among the 32 respondents (25.60%) who belonged to the age group of 26-30, the respondents were distributed equally both in crimes involving victim and no-victim. In the under 25 age category major proportion belonged to crime involving no-victim. Similar trend has been observed in other age categories except in the above 45 years category. In the above 45 category, the trend is reversed that a higher proportion of respondents (66.67%) belong to crimes involving victim than the respondents coming under the crime involving no-victim category (33.33%). It is inferred that higher proportion of aged respondents (Above 45 years) found a predominant place in crimes involving victims.

Education

There were 83 illiterate respondents (66.40) of whom 42 (50.60%) had committed crime involving victim and the remaining 41 (49.40%) had committed victimless crimes. Of the 42 literate respondents (33.60%) 19 (45.24%), respondents who had indulged in crimes involving victim and 23 (54.76%) respondents who had indulged in crimes involving no-victims. It is interesting to note that the literate population equally participated in crimes involving victim and no-victim and it suggests that there is no difference between crimes involving victim and no-victim as far as the education of the study sample is concerned.

Marital Status

When crossed the marital status with crime involving victim and no-victim showed that out of the total 63 married respondents (50.40%), 28 (44.44%) were in victim involved crimes and 35 (55.58%) had no-victims. There were 62 respondents (49.60%), who were widows, unmarried or divorced; of whom 53.23 per cent respondents committed crimes involving victim and the rest of the 46.77 per cent involved in victimless crimes. It is concluded that there is no significant difference found among the respondents who belonged to crimes involving victim and no-victim as far as unmarried, widow and separated respondents (others category) are concerned.

Caste

Out of the 62 low caste respondents, 29 (46.77%) respondents were involved in victim crimes and 33 were involved in victimless crimes. When high caste respondents totalling 63 are seen, 32 (53.33%) respondents were in crime with victims while 31 respondents had victimless crimes. It is inferred that both low and high caste respondents were distributed more or less equally in crimes involving victim and no-victim.

Religion

The 102 Hindu respondents (81.60%) were distributed more or less equally in crimes involving victim (48.04%) and no-victim (51.96%). The same trend has been observed among the non-Hindu respondents also. It is inferred that the respondents were distributed equally in both crimes involving victim and no-victim irrespective of their religion.

Monthly Income

Respondents who earned Rs. 251-500 per month were 61 in number, out of which, 32 (52.46%) had committed crimes involving no-victims. There were 26 respondents who belonged to Rs. 501-750 income category among whom 38.48 per cent respondents committed crimes involving no-victim and 61.54 per cent belonged to crimes involving no-victim. The respondents in the monthly income category of above Rs. 750 were distributed more in number in crimes involving victim than respondents committed crimes involving no-victim. It is inferred that major proportion of the respondents belonging to the income group of Rs. 251-500 were more or less equally distributed in crimes involving victim and not victim.

Residence—Before Marriage

It was observed that more respondents were belonging to the category of crime involving victim from the rural background (53) than the respondents who had committed crimes involving no-victim (40). Contrary to this, in the urban area higher proportion of respondents who committed crimes involving no-victim were observed than the respondents belongs to crimes involving victim category. It is interesting to note that the respondents with urban background were distributed triple times higher in crimes involving no-victim than in crimes involving victim category.

Residence—After Marriage

When the residence after marriage is taken into consideration the respondents were more or less equally distributed in both crimes involving victim and no-victim irrespective of their rural urban background.

III. CRIME AGAINST PERSON, PROPERTY AND MORALITY

In the following table the crime categorised into crimes against person, property and morality for the purpose of comparative analysis. It is matched with the personal profile of the respondents for further understanding.

Age

When age of the respondent is seen with the various crimes, 32 respondent come in the 26-30 years category of this fifty per cent of the respondent had committed crime against person and one fourth of each of them against property and immorality respectively. There were 27 respondents in the above 45 years age category. Which consists of 18 (66.67%) respondents with crimes against person and of 33.33 per cent involved in crimes against property. In the age category up to 25 years, among the 22 respondents, eight has committed crimes against persons, five were involved in property related crimes and nine of them were in immortal conduct. In the 31-35 years age group category (18) the respondents were distributed in crime against person (7) and property (8) and immorality (3). Among the 16 respondents in the age group of 36-40, the respondents were distributed for crimes against person (7) and crime against property (9). The age group of 41-45 years was represented by 10 respondents having 4 respondents with crimes against person and 6 other with crimes against property. It is concluded that the age increases the persons involvement in immoral crimes decreases. There is no significant difference in distribution found among these

TABLE 3.5

Crime Against Person, Property and Morality and Personal Profile

Variables	*Crime Against Persons*	*Crime Against Property*	*Crime Against Morality*	*Total*
1	**2**	**3**	**4**	**5**
Age				
Up to 25 years	08	05	09	22
	(36.37)	(22.73)	(40.90)	(100.00)
26 to 30 years	16	08	08	32
	(50.00)	(25.00)	(25.00)	(100.00)
31 to 35 years	07	08	03	18
	(43.75)	(44.44)	(16.67)	(100.00)
36 to 40 years	07	09	00	16
	(43.75)	(56.25)	—	(100.00)
41 to 45 years	04	06	00	10
	(40.00)	(60.00)	—	(100.00)
Above 45 years	18	09	00	27
	(66.67)	(33.33)	—	(100.00)
Total	**60**	**45**	**20**	**125**
Education				
Literate	19	14	09	42
	(45.24)	(33.33)	(21.43)	(100.00)
Illiterate	41	31	11	83
	(49.40)	(37.35)	(13.25)	(100.00)
Total	**60**	**45**	**20**	**120**
Marital Status				
Married	27	23	13	63
	(42.86)	(36.51)	(20.93)	(100.00)
Others (Unmarried,	33	22	07	62

(Contd.)

1	2	3	4	5
Widow, Separated)	(53.23)	(35.48)	(11.29)	(100.00)
Total	**60**	**45**	**20**	**125**
Caste				
Low Caste	28	25	09	62
	(45.16)	(40.32)	(14.52)	(100.00)
High Caste	32	20	11	63
	(45.16)	(40.32)	(14.52)	(100.00)
Total	**60**	**45**	**20**	**125**
Religion				
Hindu	49	39	14	102
	(48.04)	(38.24)	(13.72)	(100.00)
Non-Hindu	11	06	06	23
	(47.82)	(26.09)	(29.09)	(100.00)
Total	**60**	**45**	**20**	**125**
Monthly Income				
Upto Rs. 250	09	07	05	21
	(42.86)	(32.33)	(23.81)	(100.00)
Rs. 251 to Rs. 500	31	20	10	61
	(50.82)	(32.79)	(16.39)	(100.00)
Rs. 501 to Rs. 750	10	12	04	26
	(38.46)	(46.15)	(15.38)	(100.00)
Above Rs. 750	10	06	01	17
	(58.82)	(35.29)	(05.88)	(100.00)
Total	**60**	**45**	**20**	**125**
Residence (Before Marriage)				
Rural	53	28	12	93
	(56.99)	(30.11)	(12.90)	(100.00)

(Contd.)

1	2	3	4	5
Urban	07	17	12	32
	(21.86)	(53.14)	(25.00)	(100.00)
Total	**60**	**45**	**20**	**125**
Residence				
(Before Marriage)				
Rural	43	31	13	87
	(49.43)	(35.63)	(14.94)	(100.00)
Urban	14	14	05	33
	(42.42)	(42.42)	(15.15)	(100.00)
Total	**57**	**45**	**18**	**120[@]**

@ : Not applicable to unmarried.
N.B. : Figures within parentheses indicate percentage.

two types of crimes (crime against person and crime against property) as far as the age is concerned except in the above 45 years age category. It is strange to note that among the 60 respondents who have done crime against person in the study sample (125) significant proportion (30.00%) belong to above 45 age category. It is inferred that involvement of middle aged woman in crimes against person is on the increases though such crimes involve violence, toughness and aggression.

Education

Out of the 83 illiterates respondents, 41 committed crimes against person, 31 (37.35%) against property and rest of the 11 (13.26%) respondents, have 19 (45.24%) respondents involved in crimes against person, 14 (33.33%) respondents with crimes against property and 9 (21.43%) immoral respondents, among them. It is concluded that there is no significant difference in distribution found between the respondents involved in crime against person, property and immorality as far as their education is concerned. More or less proportion of literature women involved in criminal activities is a notable feature.

Marital Status

Out of the 63 (50.40%) married respondents, 27 (42.86%) had committed crimes against person, 23 (36.51%) against property and the remaining 13 (20.63%) were immoral in conduct. The 62 'other' category respondents have in their amidst, respondents committed crime against persons (53.23%), crime against property (35.48%) respondents and immoral crimes (11.29%). More or less equal percentage of distribution was found between both married and 'others' category respondents as far as their crime against person, crime against property and immorality are concerned.

Caste

Out of the 62 low caste respondents, 45.16 per cent had been sentenced for crime against person, 40.32 per cent for crime against property and 14.52 per cent of them for immorality. In high caste respondents, consisting 63 members, 50.76 per cent have committed crime against person, 31.75 per cent belonged to crime against property and 17.46 per cent belonged to immoral crimes. There is not much difference between low and high caste respondents when talking into consideration their crime against person, crime against property and immorality. It is inferred that the high caste respondents involvement in criminal activities is on the increases.

Religion

Among the 102 Hindu respondents there were 49 (46.03%) respondents involved in crimes against person, 39 (38.23%) of them were committed crimes against property and 14 (13.74%) other indulged in immoral conduct. The Non-Hindus numbering 23, have been distributed for crimes against person (47.83%), crime against property (26.08%) and for immoral indulgence as far as crime against person is concerned.

Monthly Income

Out of the 61 respondents in the income category of Rs. 251-500, 50.82 per cent were involved in crime against person, 32.79 per cent in crime against property and 16.39 per cent others in immoral conduct. There were 26 respondents under Rs. 501-750 income category have 10 (38.46%) respondents committed crimes against persons, 12 (47.16%) others in the crime against property and four respondents (15.38%) in the immorality categories. In the income group of upto Rs. 250 having 21 respondents of them 42.86 per cent respondents had done crimes against person, 33.34 per cent against property and 23.81 per cent others for immoral crimes. In the 17 respondents representing the income group of Rs. 750 and above, 10 respondents (58.82%) in crimes against person, six respondents (35.29%) in crimes against property and the remaining one respondent (5.88%) in immoral conduct. The more or less equal distribution of these three categories in the study sample, in all the income categories, indicates that there is no significant difference between income level and the nature of the crime.

Residence—Before Marriage

Rural respondents numbering 93, have 53 (57.99%) respondents committed crimes against person, 28 (30.11%) with crime against property and 12 (12.90%) in immoral offences. Among the respondents having had a urban background before marriage (32), 21.87 per cent in crime against property, and 25.00 per cent in immoral criminal conducts. In all these three types of crimes viz., crime against person, crime against property and immorality, the rural respondents were more than the urban respondents dominated in crimes against person where as the urban respondents dominated in crime against property and immorality.

Residence—After Marriage

Respondents residing in rural place after marriage were 87 in number of which 43 (49.43%) were indulged for crimes against person, 31 (35.63%) for crimes against property, and 13 (14.94%) others for immoral behaviour. The urban resident respondents (33) were distributed in crimes against person (42.42%), in crime against property (42.42%) and in immoral conduct (15.16%). More or less similar trend has been observed on crime with residence whether before or marriage or after marriage is concerned.

IV. CONVICTS AND UNDER TRIALS

In the following table the respondents were considered as prisoners and divided into convicts and under trials. An attempt has been made to cross tabulated the personal profile with the above said categories.

Age

Among the 32 respondents coming under the age group 26-30 years, 87.50 per cent were convicts and 12.50 per cent were under trials. In the 45 years and above age category (27), 77.78 per cent were convicts and 22.22 per cent were under trials. In the groups of upto 25 years 19 respondents (86.36%) were convicts and three (13.64%) were under trials. When the age group 31-35 years is seen (18), there were 61.11 per cent convicts and 38.89 per cent under trials. Among the 16 respondents, representing the age group of 36-40 years, 10 (62.50%) were convicts and 6 (37.50) were under trials. In the age group of 41-45 years, 10 respondents are seen consisting of each five convicts and under trials (Fifty per cent each). Except in the 41-45 years category, the respondents were distributed in major proportion in convict category.

TABLE 3.6

Convicts and Under Trials and Personal Profile

Variables	*Convicts*	*Under Trials*	*Total*
Age			
Up to 25 years	19	03	22
	(86.36)	(13.64)	(100.00)
26 to 30 years	28	04	32
	(87.50)	(12.50)	(100.00)
31 to 35 years	11	07	18
	(61.11)	(38.89)	(100.00)
36 to 40 years	10	06	16
	(62.50)	(37.50)	(100.00)
41 to 45 years	05	05	10
	(50.00)	(50.00)	(100.00)
Above 45 years	21	06	27
	(77.78)	(22.22)	(100.00)
Total	**94**	**31**	**125**
Education			
Literate	32	10	42
	(76.20)	(23.80)	(100.00)
Illiterate	62	21	83
	(74.70)	(25.30)	(100.00)
Total	**94**	**31**	**125**
Married Status			
Marital Status	47	16	63
	(74.60)	(25.40)	(100.00)
Others (Unmarried, Widow and Separated)	47 (75.80)	16 (24.40)	63 (100.00)
Total	**94**	**31**	**125**

(Contd.)

Variables	*Convicts*	*Under Trials*	*Total*
Monthly Income			
Upto Rs. 250	19	02	21
	(72.13)	(27.87)	(100.00)
Rs. 251 to Rs. 500	44	17	61
	(72.13)	(27.87)	(100.00)
Rs. 501 to Rs. 750	18	08	26
	(69.23)	(23.53)	(100.00)
Above Rs. 750	13	04	17
	(76.47)	(23.53)	(100.00)
Total	**94**	**31**	**125**
Residence Before Marriage			
Rural	70	23	93
	(75.27)	(24.73)	(100.00)
Urban	24	08	32
	(75.00)	(25.00)	(100.00)
Total	**94**	**31**	**125**
Residence After Marriage	**n : 90**	**n : 30**	**n : 120**
Rural	64	23	87
	(73.56)	(26.44)	(100.00)
Urban	26	07	33
	(78.79)	(21.21)	(100.00)
Total	**90**	**30**	**125@**

@ : Not applicable to unmarried.

N.B. : Figures within parentheses indicate percentage.

Education

Out of the 83 illiterate respondents, 62 were convicts (74.70%) and the remaining 21 were under trials (25.30%). Literate respondents totalling 42, have 76.20 per cent convicts and 23.80 per cent under trials amidst them. It is concluded that convicts constitute nearly three fourth of the total proportion, both among literate and illiterate respondents.

Marital Status

Married respondents who numbered 63 consisted of 47 (74.60%) convicts and 16 (25.40%) under trials. Out of the 62 others category respondents, 47 (75.80%) were convicts while 15 (24.20%) were going trial. It is obvious that convicts from three fourth of the total respondents in both married

Caste

High caste respondents are 63 in number amongst 52 (82.54%) were convicts and the remaining 11 (17.46%) were under trials. In the low caste respondents, 67.74 per cent were convicts and the rest of them were under trials (32.26%). It is concluded that convict constitute a major proportion among the high and low caste respondents.

Religion

Among the 102 Hindu respondents, there were 76 (74.50%) convicts and 26 (25.50) under trials. The 23 non-Hindu respondents consisted of more number of convicts (78.26%) than the under trials (21.27%). Convicts from a more or less equal proportion among the Hindu and non-Hindu respondents.

Monthly Income

In the income group of Rs. 251-500 per month there were 61 respondents, of them 44 (72.13%) were convicts and the other 17 (27.87%) were under trials. There were 69.23 per cent convicts and 30.77 per cent under trials in the Rs. 501-750 income group. Among the 21 respondents earning upto Rs. 250 per month, 19 (90.48%) were convicts and 9.52 per cent of them were under trials. The monthly income of 17 respondents was above Rs. 750 per month; among them 76.47 per cent were convicts while 23.53 per cent were undergoing trial. More or less same ratio of convicts and under trials as in the study sample (3 : 1), was observed in all the income categories—except upto Rs. 250 category.

Residence—Before and After Marriage

When the residence before marriage is taken into consideration there were 93 rural resident respondents, among them 75.27 per cent were convicts and 24.73 per cent of them were under trials. The urban respondents (32) were also been distributed between convicts (75.00%) and under trials (25.00%).

Among the 87 respondents residing in rural areas after marriage, 64 (73.56%) were convicts and 23 (26.44%) were under trials. Out of the 33 urban respondents, 26 (78.79%) respondents were convicted for various crimes and other 21.21 per cent were under trials. It is concluded that the same ratio of 3 : 1 for convicts and under trials as in the study sample prevails with regard to the domicile of respondents either before or after marriage.

V. SHORT-TERM AND LONG PRISONERS

The table 3.7 shows the distribution of the respondents on the basis of their length of sentences with their socio-cultural antecedents.

Age

When the age and the length of the prison term of the respondents is seem, 32 respondents aged between 26.30 years had 14 (43.75%) long-term prisoners. In the age category of above 45 years there were 16 (59.26%) long termers and 72.22 per cent short termers in the age group of 31-35 years. In the age group of 35-40 years. Out of the total 16 respondents 9 (56.25%) were long-term prisoners and 7 (43.75%) were short-

TABLE 3.7

LEGENTH OF SENTENCES AND PERSONAL PROFILE

Variables	*Long Term Prisoners*	*Short Term Prisoners*	*Total*
1	*2*	*3*	*4*
Age			
Up to 25 Years	08	14	22
	(36.96)	(63.67)	(100.00)
26 to 30 Years	14	18	32
	(43.75)	(66.25)	(100.00)
31 to 35 Years	05	13	18
	(21.78)	(72.22)	(100.00)
36 to 40 Years	09	07	16
	(56.25)	(43.75)	(100.00)
41 to 45 Years	05	05	10
	(43.75)	(56.25)	(100.00)
Above 45 Years	16	11	27
	(59.26)	(40.74)	(100.00)
Total	**57**	**68**	**125**
Age			
Up to 25 Years	08	14	22
	(36.96)	(63.67)	(100.00)
Education			
Literate	20	22	42
	(47.62)	(52.38)	(100.00)
Illiterate	37	46	83
	(44.58)	(55.42)	(100.00)
Total	**57**	**68**	**125**
Marital Status			
Married	25	38	63
	(39.68)	(60.32)	(100.00)

(Contd.)

1	2	3	4
Others (Unmarried, Widow) and Separated	32 (51.61)	30 (48.39)	62 (100.00)
Total	**57**	**68**	**125**
Caste			
Low Caste (SC, ST & MBC)	26 (41.94)	36 (58.06)	62 (100.00)
High Caste	31 (49.21)	32 (50.79)	63 (100.00)
Total	**59**	**68**	**125**
Religion			
Hindu	50 (49.01)	52 (50.99)	102 (100.00)
Non-Hindu	07 (30.43)	16 (69.57)	23 (100.00)
Total	**59**	**68**	**125**
Age			
Up to 25 Years	08 (36.96)	14 (63.67)	22 (100.00)
Education			
Literate	20 (47.62)	22 (52.38)	42 (100.00)
Monthly Income			
Up to Rs. 250	11 (52.38)	10 (47.62)	21 (100.00)
Rs. 251 to Rs. 500	26 (42.62)	35 (57.38)	61 (100.00)
Rs. 501 to Rs. 750	09 (34.62)	17 (65.38)	26 (100.00)

(Contd.)

1	2	3	4
Above Rs. 750	11 (64.71)	06 (65.38)	17 (100.00)
Total	**57**	**68**	**125**
Residence Before Marriage			
Rural	46 (49.46)	47 (50.54)	93 (100.00)
Urban	11 (34.37)	21 (65.63)	32 (100.00)
Total	**57**	**68**	**125**
Residence After Marriage	**n : 55**	**n : 65**	**n : 120**
Rural	40 (49.46)	47 (50.54)	87 (100.00)
Urban	15 (45.45)	18 (54.55)	33 (100.00)
Total	**55**	**65**	**120@**

@ : Not married to unmarried

N.B : Figures within parentheses indicate percentage.

term prisoners. Ten respondents represent the 41 to 45 year age category; out of whom each five (50.00%) belong to long-term and short-term prisoners.

It is concluded that when the age increases, the proportion of respondents in the long-term category also increases where as when the age decreases the proportion of the respondents in the short-term category increases. The involvement of order age group in serious offences led to long-term imprisonment.

Education

While seeing the education and the length of the prison,

it was seen that out of the 83 illiterate respondents, 37 (44.58%) were serving longer terms and 46 (55.42%) were short-term prisoners. The literate respondents (42) had long-term (47.62%) and short-term prisoners (52.38%). There is no significant difference in the distribution found between both illiterate and literates as far as long termers and short termers are concerned.

Marital Status

Out of the 63 married respondents, 25 were long-term prisoners and 38 were short-term prisoners. Among the 62 unmarried respondents 32 were serving longer while the remaining 30 short-term servers. It is concluded that the proportion of married respondents under the short-term category is more and there is no significant difference in distribution between the long termers and short termers as for as the 'other' category is concerned.

Caste

Low caste respondents constitute 62 members. Out of the whole, 41.94 per cent were long-term prisoners and 58.06 per cent were short-term prisoners. Out of the 63 High caste respondents there were 31 (49.21%) and 32 (50.79%) long termers and short termers respectively. It is concluded that both low caste and high caste were represented equally among long termers and short termers.

Religion

Out of the 102 Hindu respondents, more or less equal distribution was found among both long-term and short-term prisoners. Non Hindu respondents numbering 23, consisted of 7 (30.43%) long-term and 16 (69.57%) short-term prisoners.

Monthly Income

The Rs. 251 to 500 income group has 61 respondents, out of whom 26 (42.62%) were long-term prisoners and 35 (57.38%)

were short-term prisoners. Respondents who earned between Rs.501-750 numbering 26, had 34.62 per cent long-term prisoners and 65.38 per cent short termers. Respondents totalling 17 in the Rs. 750 and above income group has 64.71 per cent long termers and 35.29 per cent short termers. It is concluded that both short termers and long termers were more or less equally distributed in all the income categories. In the Rs. 501-750 category, major proportion belonged to short termers and the trend is reversed in the next income category of Rs. 750 and above, inferring that the high level of income of the respondents is associated with serious crimes.

Residence—Before Marriage

The respondents lived in rural areas before marriage were 93; among them 46 (49.46%) were serving long-term while 47 (50.54%) others were serving short-term make us to understand us that both long-term and short-term prisoners were distributed equally. But among the urban respondents (32) high proportion is seen among short termers (65.63%) than long-term prisoners (34.37%). There is no significant difference in distributed found between the rural respondents and the term of imprisonment. There is a notable difference found between the rural respondents and their term of imprisonment. It is to be understood that the urban respondents and their term of imprisonment. It is to be understood that the urban respondents constitute high proportion in short-term imprisonment, implying that their involvement is more in crimes relating to property, immorality drug etc.,

Residence—After Marriage

Respondents numbering 87 lived in rural areas after marriage; out of whom 40 (45.98%) were serving long-term prison life and 47 (54.02%) were short termers. Out of the 33 urban respondents, 15 (45.45%) were long-term prisoners and the remaining 18 (54.55%) were short-term prisoners. Both long-term prisoners and short-term prisoners were distributed more or less equally between rural and urban respondents when their residence after marriage is taken into consideration.

4
Family of Orientation

The family atmosphere or the environment where the respondent lived has a crucial role to play in the behaviour and personality of the individual. It is very essential to understand the family background of the women criminals to have an in depth understanding about them.

TABLE 4.1

Particulars of Family of Orientation

Items	*Score*	*Frequency*	*Percentage*
Family of Orientation			
Size of the Family			
Pattered & Over Crowding	(1)	75	60.00
Single Parent Home (4 + 2 & 2 or 3 + 1)	(2)	29	23.20
Intact Home (3 + 2 & 2 + 2)	(3)	21	16.80
Total		**125**	**100.00**
Total Family Members			
Up to 4		52	41.60
5 to 8		56	44.80
9 and above		84	13.60

(Contd.)

Items	*Score*	*Frequency*	*Percentage*
Family Type			
Nuclear		84	67.20
Non-Nuclear		41	32.80
Total		**125**	**100.00**
Brought Up By			
Parent		98	78.40
Grand Parent		09	07.20
Relatives		13	10.40
Others		05	04.00
Total		**125**	**100.00**
Parental Care (Score)			
Orphan	(1)	05	04.00
By Relatives	(2)	20	16.00
Single Parent	(3)	32	28.80
Both Parent	(4)	52	41.60
Idle Home Atmosphere	(5)	12	09.60
Total		**125**	**100.00**
Average Educational Score			
1 Score		53	42.40
1.10 to 4.00		31	24.80
4.10 to 5.00		19	15.20
Above 5.00		22	17.60
Drop Out From School			
Drop Out		40	32.00
No Drop Out		02	01.60
No Schooling		83	66.40
Total		**125**	**100.00**

Size of Family

For the purposes of the study of the family is divided into three and score is assigned to each category. The over crowding family (family with more than 4 children) and the family having only one child (pattered child) are given a low score of 1: family with 4 children and two or three children with single parent is assigned 2 score and family having three or two children with both parents present is assigned a score value of 3. For the purpose of assigning scores for the married respondents the family situation before her marriages is taken into consideration.

It was observed that 75 respondents (60.00%) were from pattered and over crowding category, 29 respondents (23.20%) were coming under the 2 score category and only 21 respondents (16.80%) from the third category. It is concluded that the respondents from intact home atmosphere (i.e. these assigned 3 score) are relatively low proportion in the study sample than the other two categories. Moreover the family having pattered child or over crowding have a considerable influence on the development of criminal behaviour.

More than half of the respondents were from families five or more children. When the total number of members in the family increases the problem in every sphere of life increases and ultimately leads the individual to behave deviantly.

Type of Family

In the modern world the pattern of joint family and extended family have disintegrated and 'nuclear family' comes in. Hence in the new type of family system the security and love are lacking as compared to the joint family system even though it has its quite number of merits. The data in this study revealed that nearly two third (67.20%) of the respondents (84%) belong to the nuclear family type and the remaining one third belong to 'other types of family'.

Parental Care

The socialization of children is easily facilitated when

the children are brought up by parents themselves. But due to environmental and physical factors this may not be possible in each and every family. Hence consistency in bringing up the children becomes rather not easy. In such situations the children may develop deviance or non-normative behaviour. In bringing up a child, parents play a crucial role.

In the study sample more than three-fourth of the respondents (78.40%) where brought up by parents. The respondents who were brought up by relatives, friends and neighbours were 13 (10.40%). There were also nine respondents who were brought up by their grand parents. It is important to note that there were five respondents who were orphan or street children who came away from their families when they were very young.

In order to quantity the parental care received by the respondents in the family of orientation, scores were assigned-1; followed by those brought up by relatives including grand parents, friends and neighbours-2; cared by single parent-3; taken care by both parents-4; and ideal home atmosphere-5. For the purpose of the study the ideal home atmosphere is defined here as the presence of both parents and absence of overcrowding, poverty and conflict.

Only 9.60 per cent of the respondents were brought up in the ideal home atmosphere. The highest number group (52 and 36) were brought up by both parents and single parent respectively. A considerable number of respondents (20) were brought up by their relatives, grand parents, friends and neighbours.

MEAN EDUCATION SCORE FOR FAMILY OF ORIENTATION

To obtain the mean education score of the family the following procedure was followed. Each family member was assigned a score on the basis of their educational status as follows;

Illiterate-0; primary-1; Secondary-2; above Secondary-3; Graduation-4 and professional-5. Hence the total education score for the particular family is obtained in the average score is worked out. Then to give weightage to the highest qualification attained in that family. (Since the education of one member has a bearing on other members) a new scoring pattern called 'the highest educational score pattern' was assigned by the following method, The illiterate is assigned 1; Primary 2; Secondary 3; Above Secondary 4; Graduation 5; and Professional 6.

Then the highest educational score is added to the average already worked out and thus obtained mean education score for the family.

The mean education score is classified into four categories viz., (i) those who obtained one score, (ii) 1.1 score to 5.00, and (iii) above 5.00 score.

From the table 4.1, it is observed that large proportion of the respondents ' family (42.40%) fall in the mean education of 1 which implies that all the 42.40 per cent respondents' family members were illiterate. But more than 50 per cent of the respondents' family obtained mean education score of more than 1; which conveys that in 72 respondents family either one or more members or all were literates.

It is inferred from the mean educational score of the family of orientation that the proportion of respondents, from families having literates, involving in criminal activities showed an increase.

Household Income

When the household income in the family of orientation is seen, it is clear that the mean earning of one member is worked out as Rs. 672.50. The mean income per family was estimated as Rs. 2473.83. When the number of wage earning member were seen, the mean earner per family is calculated as 3,678. The data reveal that the income of the family is not adequate to meet the expenditure of the family since the size of the family of orientation is in many cases too large. It is also inferred that in many families the non-earning member or the dependent member is more than the total earning member ultimately speaks of their low standard of life.

Drop Out

It was contended that literacy has great influence on the female criminality rate. When the literacy rate decreases the female crime rate increases and *vice versa*. Both literacy and female crime rate are negatively correlated.

With this view in mind the schooling of the respondents was taken into consideration. It was found that 68.40 per cent of them had not even entered into the school. Among the literates (25) only two completed schooling. Nearly one third (40) of the respondents were drop out from schools due to various reasons. In further analysis the activities engaged by the respondents during their school drop out period was enquire and distribution is presented in table 4.2.

TABLE 4.2

Activities Engaged in After Dropping Out of School

Activities	*Frequency*	*Percentage*
Idle at home	14	35.00
Child labour	12	30.00
Assisting in household work	06	15.00
Caring younger ones	01	02.50
Sheep rearing	01	02.50
Handicraft training	02	05.00
Early marriage (house wife)	01	02.50
Child labour & assisting at home	03	07.50
Total	**40**	**100.00**

The table 4.2 revealed that most of the respondents were idle at home after drop out from the school followed by child labours. It is also understood that these respondents were not productively used after dropped out from school.

Parental Treatment and Residential Description

Parental treatment and the residence were the respondents grow up are part of her environment which plays a dominant role in her character molding. To understand whether the treatment received by the respondents is substantial or low, when compared to the male counterpart in the family were questioned so as to have a knowledge about the preferential treatment if any shown.

TABLE 4.3

Parental Treatment and Residential Description

Items	*Frequency*	*Percentage*
Treatment By Parents		
Unequal Treatment	66	52.80
No difference in treatment	42	33.60
Do not know/ Not applicable	17	13.60
Total	**125**	**100.00**
Preferential Treatment Felt		
Being as 'Female'	69	55.20
Preferential Treatment	39	31.20
No Preferential shown	17	13.60
Population Density		
Over populated	57	45.60
Not Over populated	64	51.20
Not applicable	04	03.20
Total	**125**	**100.00**
Room Facilities		
Narrow/Congested Rooms	99	79.20

(Contd.)

Items	*Frequency*	*Percentage*
Enough Spacious Rooms	22	17.60
Not applicable	04	03.20
Total	**125**	**100.00**
Space and House Environment		
Lack of and/or congested space	102	81.60
Spacious	19	15.20
Not applicable	04	03.20
Total	**125**	**100.00**
Poverty and Family		
Brought up in Poverty	96	76.80
Not in Poverty	25	20.00
Not Applicable	04	03.20
Total	**125**	**100.00**
Criminal Risk During Childhood		
Exposure to Criminal Risk	14	11.20
Not in Criminal Risk	109	87.20
Do not know	02	01.60
Total	**125**	**100.00**
Parental Conflict		
Conflicting and/or Quarrelsome Parents	43	34.40
No Conflicts among Parents	78	62.40
Not Applicable	04	03.20
Total	**125**	**100.00**

Preferential Treatment

It was observed that in 66 respondents' families that the treatment given to both male and female was equal. There were one third of the respondents (33.60%) who felt difference in treatment. It includes both low and high level of treatments compared with male siblings. Among the 42 respondents who experienced equal treatment only three respondents were given more preference than their male counterparts.

In an another enquiry, the preferential treatment shown to male rather than female was obtained. More than half of the respondents (55.20%) admitted that preferential treatment in love, care, security, education and employment was given to male counterparts in her family of orientation by their parents. In 31.20 per cent cases no such preference was experienced by the respondents. It is also interesting to note that 13.60 per cent (17) of the respondents were not aware whether preferential treatment was given or not.

Residential Description

Studies in the field of women crime revealed that over population, narrow/congested rooms, poverty, parental conflict, criminal risk during childhood and sibling position are contributory factors for the development of criminal behaviour among women. Hence an attempt has been made to investigate these area in detail.

Population

A family having more than four children is defined as 'over populated' for the purpose of the study. More than half of the respondents (51.20%) were from families of 'not over populated' and 45.60 per cent of them over populated families. For four respondents this classification would not apply since they are orphans.

Room Facilities

As far as the available room facilities are concerned majority of the respondents (79.20%) felt that they have lived in narrow and congested rooms. Only 17.60 per cent (22) of the respondents lived in spacious rooms.

House Environment

When their space and house environment are noted majority of the respondents (81.60%) admitted that their houses did not have enough space to live and only 15.20 per cent of the respondents felt that their houses were spacious enough.

Poverty

Poverty plays a crucial role in the development of criminal behaviour. Majority of respondents (76.80%) totalling 90 confessed that they were brought up in conditions of poverty and only 25 cases (20.00%) escaped from the clinches of poverty in their family of orientation.

Expsoure to Criminal Risk during Childhood

It was intended to know whether there were any chances of exposure to criminal risk during childhood. Majority the respondents (87.20%) expressed that they were not exposed to such situations and only 11.20 per cent (14) of the respondents were exposed to criminal risk during their childhood days.

Parental Conflict

Parental conflict/quarrelsome nature of parents have some bearing on the criminality among females have been observed by various studies. In the present study, 78 respondents' (62.40%) parents had no conflict among them and only 34.40 per cent (43) respondents experienced that their parents had conflict. The reasons for conflict are given in table 4.4.

When the response for conflict were traced it was observed that 15 respondents parent had conflict/quarrels due to their own deviance or involvement in criminal activities. The various other reasons attributed are poverty

(18), property dispute (19) and prostitution (3). In some cases the reasons are multiple in nature.

TABLE 4.4

Reasons for Conflict Between Respondents' Parents

Reasons for Conflict	*Frequency**
Poverty	18
Due to deviance	19
Property dispute	03
Prostitution	03

* Multiple response

Sibling Position

In table 4.5 siblings position of the respondents were distributed.

TABLE 4.5

Sibling Position

Sibling Position	*Frequency*	*Percentage*
Only Child	08	06.40
First Born	36	28.80
Second Born	27	21.60
Middle Born	40	21.60
Last Born	14	11.20
Total	**125**	**100.00**

* multiple response

It was contended by the researches that the second born or the middle born are aggressive so-as to obtain rights and facilities on par with the first born. Sometimes deviances is the means to reach these objectives. Hence considerable proportion of the deviants are second born or middle born.

In the present study it was observed that majority of 67 respondents (53.60%) were second born and middle born. Moreover a considerable proportion of respondents (28.80%) were the first born child followed by last born 14(11.20%) and there were eight respondents who were the only child of the family.

It was to be argued that sibling position had no significant role to play as far as criminal involvement is concerned. Since the second born or middle born constitutes more or less equal proportion with other positioned children.

Financial Difficulties

To understand the economic problem whether the income of the family is adequate or not to meet the family requirements was questioned.

It revealed that majority of 114 respondents (91.23%) reiterated that the family income is not adequate and hence they tried various methods to balance it.

It revealed that majority of 114 respondents (91.23%) reiterated that the family income is not adequate and hence they tried various methods to balance it.

There were 52 respondents who got loan on interest mortgaged jewels and properties to balance the situation. But for 31 respondents they had not indulge in criminal activities to earn money in order to balance the economic crisis in the family.

Financial Management

When the financial management is not done effectively the family may face economic problems. Hence the management of finance in family needs an effective person to perform. When the source of income is not adequate then the economic crisis arises.

TABLE 4.6

Financial Difficulties and Management

Items	*Frequency*	*Percentage*
Whether Income Adequate	**n : 125**	
Inadequate Income	114	91.23
Adequate Income	011	08.77
Ways of Balance Management*		
Loan (On jewel, property and interest)	052	
Help from parents/friends and others	023	
Earning from criminal activities	031	
Financial Management in Respondents Family		
Financial Management		
By Respondents	037	29.60
By Husband	068	54.40
By Relatives	011	08.80
Both by Respondent and Husband	009	07.20

* : Multiple Response

In the study the role of the financial manager was performed by the husbands in more than half of the families (54.40%). Due to reasons like bad habits of the husbands, unproductive husbands, extravagance of the other family members the respondents were in majority of the cases forced to take the role of the financial manager. This new role requires some more additional functions to perform and specifically to meet the financial demands of the family. This study shows that there 37 respondents (29.60%) who played the role of the financial manager before they come to the prison. The role of managing financial affairs of the family may open gate way whether directly or indirectly to involve in anti-social activities. It is strange to note that there were 8.80 per cent of the respondents whose family were managed by other relatives than her husband. These situations also make the individual to have conflict on financial matters.

Details of Guardian

Guardian in the place of parents can only be a substitute and not the parent. The concern, love and care along with socializing the children given by parents give a better result than if it is given by a guardian. In many cases the physical absence, separation, broken home atmosphere force children to be brought up by a guardian. In the present study also some of the respondents were brought up by guardians and it is dealt with in detail in the proceeding analysis.

Profiles of the Guardian

It is essential to understand the profile of the guardian since each has a bearing on the children who were brought up by them.

TABLE 4.7

Details of Guardian

Details of Guardian	*Frequency*	*Percentage*
Illiterate	021	91.23
Primary	003	11.11
Secondary	002	07.41
Professionals	001	03.70
Total	**027**	**100.00**
Occupation of Guardian		
Illegal activities	002	07.41
Unemployed/irregular/coolie	020	74.08
Agri Coolie/Traditional occupation	002	07.41
Total	**027**	**100.00**

Children brought up by other than parents have their influence on the behaviour of the individual. There were 27 respondents who were brought up by other than their parents. Among them majority of 21 respondents' (77.78%) guardian were illiterates. When their occupation is concerned majority of 20 respondents' guardians were unemployed and in irregular employment and coolies.

It was found that majority of the guardian were illiterates and employed in irregular and menial occupations and even some of them were unemployed. It is crystal clear that these families must be in a low economic status with economic deprivation, malnutrition, conflicts on economic grounds which added more to the development of the criminal behaviour among the respondents.

5
Family of Procreation and Details of Husbands

It is in the family of procreation women occupy the new roles and status as wife, mother, householder, care taker etc. It is also said that a new life has started for the individual when she entered into another family by way of wedlock. The new social roles and status are equally important for the development of normal social being. In this chapter attempts have been made to bring forth the details regarding family particulars, relationship with other members and treatment received from other members by the respondents.

Size

It is understood from Table 5.1 that in 32 respondents' (26.67%) families there were only two members i.e. only the respondent and her husband and in 24 respondents' family (28.23%) they had only one child and in 27 respondents family (22.50%) the total family members were four. It is inferred that the size of the family of orientation. It is to note that most of the respondents (96.00%) had been convicted after their marriage. This may be due to the reason that marital maladjustments, conflict with husbands and in-laws whether directly or indirectly influence the behaviour of the respondents.

TABLE 5.1

Details of Family Procreation

Items	*Frequency*	*Percentage*
Size		
2 Members	32	26.67
3 Members	24	28.33
4 Members	27	22.50
5 Members	15	10.00
Above 5 Members	15	12.50
Total	**120**	**100.00**
Average Education Score		
1 Score	41	34.17
1.1 to 4.00	34	28.33
4.1 to 5.00	18	15.00
Above 5.00	27	22.50
Total	**120**	**100.00**

Household Income

It is observed from the data collected that the mean income per earning member of the family of procreation is worked out as Rs. 705.28. The mean income per family is estimated as Rs. 1826.80. The mean earner per family is 2.59. These data inferred that though the income level of the family of procreation is higher than the family of orientation the income is not adequate to meet the family requirements in the sense that most of the respondents belonged to the middle age group in which their family have large number of dependent members. Another contributory factors reported by the respondents to support the contention that the household income is not adequate is that most of the husbands had bad habits such as alcoholic, drug addict etc., (analysed in the later part) in which a considerable part of the income spent on these items.

Education

The educational status shows that though 41 respondents' family had no education, the other 79 respondents' family had either one or more members educated. A considerable portion (22.50%) in the above 5.00 mean education score category implies that the level of education in the family of procreation is greater than the level of education in the family of orientation.

TABLE 5.2

Mean Education Scopre Nature of Crime Committed

Nature of Crime	*Education*			*Total*
	Illiterate n : 41	*Minimal Education n : 34*	*Better Education n : 45*	*n : 120*
Type I				
Murder	17	16	21	54
Non-murder	24	18	24	66
Type II				
Involves Victim	18	18	22	58
Involves no-victim	23	16	23	62
Type III				
Against Person	18	18	21	57
Against Property	16	09	20	45
Against Morality	07	07	04	18
Type IV				
Long Termers	15	15	25	55
Short Termers	26	19	20	65
Type V				
Convicts	34	22	34	90
Undertrails	07	12	11	30

Education and Nature of Crime

For the purpose of comparative analysis the mean family education score has been classified into three as follows:— Those whose mean family education score is 1, Minimal education—Those mean family education score is between 1.1 to 4.0 and Better education—Those who obtained more than 4.1 mean family education score.

It is observed that the illiterate—family constitute 41; minimal educated family 34 and better educated family—45. Hence the significant number of the respondents were from better educated family of procreation.

Among the 54 respondents who involved in crime relating to murder 21 were from better educated families. When non-murder category is taken into consideration there were a equal proportion of respondents both from illiterates (24) and better educated (24) families.

Among the better educated family (45) there were more or less equal proportion of respondents who indulged in crimes involving victim and no-victim. The crimes involving no-victim category respondents had equal representation from both illiterate and better educated families.

Among the 57 respondents who committed crime against persons, highest proportion of respondents (21) were from better educated family and equal proportion of respondents were (18) from both illiterate and minimal educated families. With regard to the immorality offenders both illiterate and minimal educated families have equal proportion (7) and only small portion of respondents (4) belong to better educated family.

Among the 90 convicts studied, equal number of respondents (34) were from both illiterate and better educated family. The undertrial category has more or less equal proportion of 12 and 11 respondents from both minimal educated families respectively.

Among the 55 long-term prisoners nearly half (25) of them were from better educated families and an equal proportion (15) were from both illiterate and minimal educated families.

It is inferred from the table 5.2 that the involvement of persons in crime from educated family is increasing day by day. More over there is not much difference between the type of crime committed and the average educational level of the family of procreation.

Marriage Particulars

Marriage is one of the important social institutions in which human relations are deeply involved. It is also a complex social system. In the traditional Hindu family the status of wife is considered inferior and mostly they depend upon their husbands and/or parents-in-law. In many studies it was contended that marital adjustments, conflict over sex, illegal contact of the women or her husbands were often found responsible in one way or the other in making women indulge in crime. Hence an attempt has been made to probe the marriage related issues in detail.

Inter-Caste Marriage

The caste system in India was traditionally more powerful and controlled the people marrying from other caste. Nowadays, due to education, industrialization, urbanization and civilization, the caste barrier is disappearing and inter-caste marriages are taking place. Though apparently changes are seen. In many cases the inter-caste marriage have taken place without the contsent of the parents. This often results in lack of security from parents both socially and economically resulting in conflicts, failures and broken homes. In the criminal context conflict and broken home are the contributory factors in crime. Hence the caste of the husbands were analyzed.

TABLE 5.3

Marriage Particulars

Items	*Frequency*	*Percentage*
Husbands' Caste		
Same caste of the respondents	100	83.33
Different caste than the respondents	20	16.67
Total	**120***	**100.00**
Marriage Particulars		
Respondents		
Married once	108	90.00
Married more than once	12	10.00
Total	**120***	**100.00**
Husband		
Married once	85	70.83
Married more than once	35	29.17
Total	**120***	**100.00**
Type of Marriage		
(Respondent latest marriage)		
Arranged Marriage	82	68.33
Love Marriage	38	31.67
Total	**120***	**100.00**
Status of Marriage		
(Respondent latest marriage)		
Legal Marriage	83	69.17
Illegal Marriage (contact)	37	30.83
Total	**120***	**100.00**

In the present study there were 20 respondents who married outside their caste. Further prove into the caste of the husband whether high or low in comparison of the respondents gave the following result.

Among the married respondents majority of them (83.33%) married in their own caste and only 16.67 per cent married their husbands from other caste. In the traditional Indian family the inter-caste marriages are considered to be 'less appreciable though industrialization and urbanization have accelerated at a much higher rate'. Hence the inter-caste marriages faced certain hardships from the family and society. It is also understood that 16.67 per cent respondents who had entered into inter-caste marriage majority of them, faced problems both from the family of procreation and family of orientation. The problem is much more serious both the respondents and husbands when they married their partners lower than their caste. The table explains whether the caste of the husband is lower or higher than the respondents.

TABLE 5.4

Caste of the Husbands in other than the Respondents

Husbands' Caste	*Frequency*	*Percentage*
Lower than the respondent	13	65.00
Higher than the respondent	07	35.00
Total	**20***	**100.00**

* Only twenty respondents married other caste people.

It is revealed from the table 5.4 that among the 20 inter-caste marriages 13 husbands belonged to lower caste than the respondents and the seven others belong to higher caste than the respondent. It is kept in mind that in the traditionally male dominated Indian society, marrying lower caste bride is considered low than marrying high caste bride. In the present study the majority of the respondents married higher caste bride room than their caste make us to understand that the problems involved in it. In such families the conflict and quarrels may be frequent and which might have added stress and strain to the respondent.

Type of Marriage and Status of Marriage

Apparently there are two types of marriages; one is on the basis of the choice of the partners and another is on the basis of the choice of the families that enter into the marriage contract; they are love marriage and arranged marriage. As far as the status of the marriage is concerned it is based on the legality of the marriage whether it is legal or other than legal. It is also be understood that a love marriage can be legal or illegal so as for arranged marriage too. Many love marriages are done without the consent of the parents and parents in-law and also many of the arranged marriages are done without the consent of bride and the groom. Hence in both cases there are more possibilities for conflicts maladjustments. Hence an attempt is made to distribute the respondents on the basis of the type and status of their marriage.

TABLE 5.5

Type of Marriage and Status of Marriage

Type of Marriage	*Status of Marriage*		*Total*
	Legal Marriage	*Other than Legal Marriage*	
Love Marriage	11 (13.25)	27 (72.97)	38 (31.67)
Arranged Marriage	72 (86.74)	10 (27.03)	82 (68.33)
Total	**83** **(100.00)**	**37** **(100.00)**	**120** **(100.00)**

In the table 5.5 the 'other than legal marriage' includes concubinism, cohabitation etc. It is understood that among the 82 arranged marriage that took place majority (86.74%) were legal and the rest 10 marriages (27.03%) were other than legal marriages. Among the 38 love marriages majority (27) of them were other than legal, and other 11 were legal.

Frequency of Marriage: A Comparison

The frequency of marriage shows frequent quarrels, conflict, maladjustments and misunderstanding either on the part of the respondents or husband or both. If a person marries more than one time or many time it is an indication of his or her maladjustment or lack of understanding with the first married partner. Hence an attempt has been made to estimate the frequency of the marriage.

TABLE 5.6

A Comparison of Frequency Marriage

Respondent	*Husband*		*Total*
	Ist. Marriage	*Not Ist. Marriage*	
First Marriage	81 (95.29)	27 (77.14)	108 (90.00)
Not First Marriage	04 (04.71)	08 (22.86)	12 (10.00)
Total	**85 (100.00)**	**35 (100.00)**	**120 (100.00)**

When the latest marriage of the respondents is analysed it is observed that it is the first marriage for 81 respondents and their husbands; they have married more than one time. There were 27 respondents married their partner who had been already married (or for the 27 husbands it was not their first marriage).

It is peculiar to note that for four respondents the present marriage was not the first marriage; but for the husbands it was the first one. There were also eight respondents and husbands who entered into the marriage contract not for the first time.

Comparison of Type of Marriage and Nature of Crime

With the view to have a comparative analysis the type of marriage has been crossed with the nature of crime committed by the respondents and the results are given in table 5.7.

TABLE 5.7

Type of Marriage and Nature of Crime

Nature of Crime	*Type of Marriage*		*Total*
	Love Marriage n : 38	*Arranged Marriage n : 82*	*n : 120*
Type I			
Murder	13	41	54
Non-murder	25	41	66
Type II			
Involves Victim	15	43	58
Involves no-victim	23	39	62
Type III			
Against Person	14	43	57
Against Property	14	31	45
Against Morality	10	08	18
Type IV			
Long Termers	15	40	55
Short Termers	23	42	65
Type V			
Convicts	30	60	90
Undertrails	08	22	30

In the murder and non-murder category the respondents, whose marriage was an arranged one were equally distributed. For the respondents who had love marriage majority (25 out of 38) of them belong to the non-murder category. More or less same trend has been observed in the crime involving victim and no-victim categories.

There was a considerable difference in distribution seen between love and arranged marriage respondents belonging to convict and undertrials category. Among the respondents from arranged marriage category (82), majority of them were long-term prisoners (60) and the rest were short-term, marriage was arranged involved mostly in crimes relating to imprisonment is relatively higher.

Age at Marriage

It is observed that for majority of the respondents their first marriage took place at the age of 15 to 18 years. Though the Indian Marriage Acts, fixed the minimum age for female as above 18 years. This is one of important reasons that these females were not mentally and physically matured enough to cop up with the new roles and status assigned to them through their marriage in the family of procreation. It is also a sorry state that considerable proportion (27) of respondents married on or before they attained the age of 14 years. To probe further, the age or first and second marriage of both respondents and husbands, the table 5.8 has been constructed.

It is obviously strange to observe the majority of the husbands (43) married for the first time at the age of 25 to 27 years. More or less equal number of (41) husbands married on or before they attained 21 years. It is inferred that females were given in marriage early and males were adequately given time to marry. In one way it is inferred that females were forced to given to marriage by their parents at an early age so as to relieve themselves from the burden of keeping the females in the family of orientation. These situation added further stress in the minds of the female to develop deviant behaviour.

TABLE 5.8

Age at Marriage(s)

Age at Marriage	*Frequency*	*Percentage*
Respondent		
First Marriage		
Upto 14 years	27	22.50
15 to 16 years	30	25.00
17 to 18 years	28	23.33
19 to 20 years	21	17.50
Above 20 years	14	11.67
Total	**120***	**100.00**
Second Marriage		
Upto 20 years	03	02.50
21 to 25 years	03	02.50
Above 25 years	06	05.00
Not applicable	108	91.20
Total	**120**	**100.00**
Husband		
First Marriage		
Upto 21 years	45	37.50
22 to 24 years	15	12.50
25 to 27 years	43	35.83
28 to 30 years	15	12.50
Above 30 years	06	05.00
Total	**120***	**100.00**
Second Marriage		
Upto 24 years	03	02.50
25 to 27 years	08	06.67
28 to 30 years	09	07.50
Above 30 years	77	64.20
Total	**120***	**100.00**

* Among the 125 sample only 120 are married and other 5 are unmarried.

Second and third Marriage

There were 12 respondents married for the second time and three respondents married for the third time. In the Indian context marrying more than one time for the male is some what approved, but if a female marries more than once it is viewed as strain and awful. In the present study also the number of husbands who married the second time (43) and third time (6) were more than the respondents who married second and third time.

Age at Marriage Comparison

Age at marriage of respondents and husbands are compared in the proceedings analysis taking into consideration their latest marriages with a view to understand the age difference between the respondents and husbands.

TABLE 5.9

Age at Marriage: Comparison

Respondents	*Husband*					*Total*
	Upto 21	*22-24*	*25-27*	*28-30*	*Above 30*	
Upto 14	09	03	10	03	02	27
15-18	15	01	12	03	00	31
17-18	10	06	07	02	02	27
19-20	06	05	08	00	02	21
Above 20	01	00	06	07	00	14
Total	**41**	**15**	**43**	**15**	**06**	**120**

Among the 120 respondents majority of them got married on or before they attained 20 years age. The age of the husbands showed a strange distribution that a considerable proportion of 41 to 43 belong to upto 21 years and 25 to 27 years category respectively.

Among 27 respondents who got married before attained 14 years, their major number of husbands (10) belong to 25-27 years age category. It showed on age difference of 11 to 13 years respondents and husbands.

It is inferred that there is a significant difference between the age at marriage of respondents and husbands. The high age difference between the spouses in many at time is identified with lack of understanding, conflict over sex matters and maladjustments in the family hence, added further stress and strain on the respondents.

Illegal Relationship

Illegal relationships or extramarital relationships often lead to conflict, quarrelling, illtreatment and broken homes for those who involved in it and also for those whose spouse was involved in it. For example, if a husband had illegal contact with other than his wife; his wife may face problems by way of illtreatment and quarrelling and if a female had illegal contact then she will be illtreated both by her husband and parents-in-law. Hence an attempt has been made to probe the illegal relationships of the respondents and husbands.

TABLE 5.10

Illegal Relationship

Illegal Relationship	*Frequency*	*Percentage*
For Respondents		
Had illegal contact	33	26.40
Had no illegal contact	92	73.60
Total	**125**	**100.00**
For Husbands		
Had illegal contact	56	46.67
Had no illegal contact	64	53.33
Total	**120**	**100.00**

It is revealed from the table 5.10 that both respondents (26.40%) and husbands (46.67%) had illegal contact. It clearly shows that the degree of maladujstments and conflict between the respondents and husbands, which many a time lead to behave anti-socially. To have an indepth understanding, the respondents and husbands were compared in regard to their illegal contact with other persons in table 5.11.

TABLE 5.11

Illegal Relationship of Respondent and Husbands

Respondent	*Husband*		*Total*
	Illegal Contact	*No Illegal Contact*	
Illegal Contact	18 (32.14)	13 (20.31)	31 (25.83)
No Illegal Contact	38 (67.86)	51 (79.69)	89 (74.17)
Total	**56** **(100.00)**	**64** **(100.00)**	**120*** **(100.00)**

* In the total sample of 125, 5 are Unmarried; among the 5 Unmarried 2 respondents had illegal contact.

It is revealed that there were 33 respondents and 56 husband had illegal contact. There were only 51 respondents and husbands who had no illegal relations with anybody. Among the 89 respondents who had no illegal contact, their 38 husbands had illegal contact. It is interesting to note that there were 18 respondents and husbands had illegal contact out side the wedlock.

Added to this five unmarried respondents had illegal contact with other married persons. It is inferred that marital maladjustments plays a major role as far as the reasons for the criminal behaviour is concerned. It has either direct or indirect influence on the deviant behaviour of the respondents.

Conflict and Illtreatment in Husband's Family

There are various grounds in which both husband and wife can have conflict. When both are not adjusting themselves then conflict is the result. Many a time when the conflict is not resolved it leads to further problems and may also result in deviant behaviour among the individuals. Hence an attempt has been made to analyse the conflict between husband and respondents.

In many families the married women are treated very badly for various reasons in which they have no control over them. Lack of adjustment, not coping with the expectations of the husbands and in-laws, quarrelsome nature of the members of the family of procreation, etc., lead the female to be illtreated by the husbands and other family members. Illtreatment adds further stress and strain on the part of the respondents lead them to involve in antisocial activities.

TABLE 5.12

Conflict and Illtrement

Conflict and Illtreatment	*Frequency*	*Percentage*
Conflict with Husband		
Conflict existed	66	55.00
No Conflict existed	54	45.00
Total	**120***	**100.00**
Illtreatment in Husband's Family		
Felt by Respondent		
By Husband	61	50.83
By parents-in-law	28	23.33
By in-laws	19	15.83
Husband's other relatives	17	14.17
Total	**120**	**100.00**

More than half of the respondents (55%) had conflict with their husbands for one reason or the other. However 45 per cent respondents contended that they had no illegal conflict with their husbands.

Among the 120 married respondents half of them (50.83%) were illtreated by their husbands due to various reasons. Moreover nearly one fourth of the respondents (23.33%) were illtreated by their parents-in-law. There were also 15.83 per cent respondents who faced illtreatment from their in-laws. A considerable proportion (14.17%) of respondents were also illtreated by their husbands' other relatives. When the individual is exposed it illtreatment by these agencies it may make her frustrated, aggressive and violent which takes any form of deviance if the situation permits. The various types of illtreatment received by the respondents were attempted to murder, beating, scolding, giving no food, not permitted to meet the husband, illtreating their children, house imprisonment, repeatedly asking for dowry etc.

Husband' Details

The role of the husband in the family of procreation has direct influence on the respondents. If the husband performs his role and responsibilities in an reactive manner, adjusts with family environment, productive, without any bad habits and not of conflicting nature is an asset to any family and so is the case for wife too. But in many cases the husbands are not fulfilling their family role and functions resulting in conflicts and quarrels ultimately leading to crisis in the family in all spheres such as social, economical and familial. Hence in the present study attempts have been made to find out the details of the husbands, their income, their habits, whether having illegal contacts, whether affected by chronic illness and whether involving in criminal activities, were studied.

TABLE 5.13

Details of Husbands

Items	*Frequency*	*Percentage*
Husbands Occupation	**n : 74**	
Illegal activities	10	13.51
Unemployed/Coolie	14	18.92
Agri coolie/traditional work	03	04.05
Skilled/technical service	37	50.00
Trade/agriculturist	10	13.51
Husbands' Income		
Upto Rs. 500	22	29.73
Rs. 501 to Rs. 1000	28	37.84
Above Rs. 1000	24	32.43
Total	**74**	**100.00**
Mean income : Rs. 746.80		
Standard Deviation : Rs. 1274.78		
Husbands' Habit	**n : 120**	
Alcoholic	74	61.67
Drug addict	35	29.17
Having illegal contact	52	43.33
Affected by chronic illness	22	18.33
Involved in criminal activities	43	35.83
Had criminal record	38	31.67
Present Residence of Husbands'	**n : 120**	
Native Place	59	49.17
Prison	17	14.17
Do not know	07	05.83
Not applicable	37*	30.83

* Includes 28-Dead; 2-Murdered by others and 7-Murdered by Respondents.

When the monthly income of the husbands is estimated there were 28 respondents' husbands (37.84%) who earned an income ranging from Rs. 501 to 1000. There were 24 and 22 husbands whose income ranged from Rs. 1000 and above and upto Rs. 5000 categories respectively. The mean income of the husbands' is Rs. 746.80, with a standard deviation of Rs. 1274.78 and it ranges from Rs. 200 to Rs. 10,000.

In comparison with the income of the respondents it is inferred that the income level of the husbands are relatively higher than the respondents though not adequate to meet the family expenditure. It was also understood that only 74 husbands out of 120 were successfully employed in various occupations.

The bad habits, illegal contact and involving in criminal activities have considerable influence on the respondents and the family. In various studies the bad habits of the husbands have directly influenced the respondents in arising out of their husbands' bad habits. The involvement of husbands in criminal activities have direct influence on the wife to indulge in crime. More over the criminal husbands also forces their wives to do crime in which the wife play the role of an accomplice to her husband. Hence the habits and behaviour were analysed in detail.

Among the (120) husbands 74 of them (61.67%) were alcoholic and 35 (out of 120) were addicted to drugs. There were 22 husbands (18.33%) affected by chronic illness and 35.83 per cent were involved in criminal activities as confessed by the respondents and among them only 31.67 per cent (38 out of 120) had criminal record.

It is inferred that in many cases the respondents played the role of an accomplice along with husbands while he committed the crime and convicted for the same. The bad habits of the husbands and chronic illness make the family suffer economically and hence the respondents were forced to play the role of the husband in earning and feeding the themselves in criminal activities. In crimes like illicit trading, when the husband is convicted, the wife continue the husband's trading and got convicted.

Present Details of the Husband

In order to understand what the husbands were doing at the time of study, the respondents were enquired about the present position of their husbands and the collected responses are distributed in the table.

It is noted that there were 30.83 per cent of the husbands (37) who were not alive. Among them seven were murdered by the respondents and two of them were murdered by others. A considerable proposition of husbands (17) were sentenced in the prison. In many cases of murder related crimes both husbands and the respondents were convicted. It is also interesting to note that there were 7 respondents who do not know where their husbands are at present. Among them five husbands are searched by the court of law for their criminal conduct. The other two cases left the family for the fear of the society and stigma attached due to their wives' criminal behaviour.

6
Crimes Committed

I. CHILDHOOD CRIMINAL BEHAVIOUR

In order to find out whether during childhood the respondents were engaged in criminal conduct the following analysis is made. Further analysis was also made to estimate whether their close relatives or childhood friends have criminal record. The results are distributed in the table below.

TABLE 6.1

Childhood Criminal Behaviour

Childhood Criminal Behaviour	*Frequency*	*Percentage*
Involving in criminal activity along with parent/guardian.	3 (125)	02.40
Trained during childhood in criminal activities.	2 (125)	01.60
Respondents' childhood friend had criminal record.	25 (125)	20.00
Respondents' close relatives had criminal record.	45 (125)	36.00

N.B. : Figures in parentheses indicate the total number of respondents.

It was observed that there were 2.40 per cent of the respondents (3) who have engaged in criminal activities along with their parents or guardians during their childhood days.

More over two respondents were also trained for the purpose.

It was observed that 20 per cent and 36.00 per cent of the respondents admitted that their friends and close relatives respectively record.

II. CRIMES COMMITTED

Since time immemorial crime is with us. It is only in the recent past, crime has drawn much attention and seriously looked into due to the drastic increase in male and female crime rate. In the earlier days people were of the opinion that crime was only a male affair. The women were treated as less aggressive, more moral. It is very recently that women have been occupied position in criminological literature as subjects to be studied. Industrialization, urbanization and modernization throw ways to women to expose themselves to the outside world which brought them many chances to engage in criminal activities.

Nowadays women are engaged in wide variety of crimes. They are proven equal in line as with men in committing crimes. Violent crimes requires physical toughness, aggression are not only male affairs nowadays. Hence in the following analysis the nature of crime committed by the respondents are brought out.

Nature of Crime Committed

Women are engaged in wide variety crimes as men do. In the present study also women engaged in various crimes as distributed in table 6.2.

It was observed that major proportion of the respondents (50) were murderers, among them two respondents committed triple murder, one committed double murder and other two respondents had been involved in dowry murders. The murder related crimes category consists of respondents involved in attempted murder (3), accomplice in murder (2) and one attempted for self immolation.

TABLE 6.2

Distribution of Respondents by Type of Crime Committed

Nature of Crime Committed	*Frequency*	*Percentage*
Murder	50	40.00
Murder related Crimes	06	04.80
Illicit distillation	24	19.20
Immorality	20	16.00
Drug related Crimes	14	11.20
Theft	05	04.00
Smuggling	02	01.60
Quarrelling	03	02.40
Kidnapping	01	00.80
Total	**125**	**100.00**

Little less than one fifth of the respondents (19.20%) were involved in illicit distillation and another one sixth of them (16.00%) imprisoned for immorality.

Among those who involved in drug related crimes (14), there were drug traffickers (8) and drug peddlers (6). Those who committed theft was 4.00 per cent. The various other crimes the respondents involved were quarrelling (3), sandalwood smuggling respectively.

Cause of Crime

It is very difficult to identify a particular cause for a particular criminal activity. Sometimes a specific factor in a particular situation becomes the cause for a specific type of criminal behaviour. Hence in the analysis of causation, possibilities for different kinds of interpretations are to be kept in mind and one has to carefully discern the real cause or causes for a given criminal behaviour.

TABLE 6.3

Causes for Crime Committed

	Causes	*Frequency **
I.	**Economical Causes**	**155**
	Poverty	047
	Unemployment	051
	Low income	048
	Property dispute	009
II.	**Social Causes**	**075**
	Family responsibility	064
	Too many children	006
	Local political quarrel	003
	Dowry dispute	002
III.	**Personal Causes**	**123**
	Self defence	009
	Emotional reasons	017
	Conflict with daughter	001
	For survival	004
	Vengeance	002
	To make more money	042
	To lead a luxury life	048
IV.	**Illtreatment**	**018**
	Illtreatment by husband	005
	Bad habits of husband	005
	Illtreatment of relatives	006
	Illtreatment of employer	002
V.	**Illegitimacy**	**031**
	Husband illegal contact	017
	Respondents illegal contact	011
	Illegal contact of dear and near ones	003

Mean Number of Causes : 3.21

* Multiple response

The causes for criminal activity were enquired from the respondents. The responses were collected and listed in a sequence. For the purpose of classification they were then classified under five major headings. The detailed study of these causes follows in the succeeding pages.

(i) Economical Causes

Under the economic causes, the respondents have given some reasons for their criminal activity. As it is widely believed unemployment, low income and poverty go hand in hand, and they lead an individual to resort to criminal means in order to achieve their goals. This finding has been supported by many other studies conducted in India on women criminality.

The present study also confirms it. Unemployment was cited by 51 respondents as a reason for their crime. Low income, which also one of the factors induces the criminal activity has been endorsed by 48 respondents. Poverty is the major popular propagator of crime in the human society, is one of the causes for 47 respondents. Property dispute had lead 9 respondents to commit criminal act.

(ii) Social Causes

Social causes cited by the respondents were few. The role of the family responsibility, earning money, taking care of the family, managing the affairs of the family, decision making etc., are normal course carried out by the male member of the family as far as the Tamil Nadu's cultural context is concerned. In some circumstances, due to various factors, these role performances are shouldered by the female members adding further stress and strain on them apart from their role as the mother and the householder. This new role of family responsibility some time motivate the females to engage in anti-social means to achieve their end. In the present study, the responsibility for family has motivated 64 respondents to indulge in crime. Other factors that causes the crime are dowry dispute—a particular phenomenon in India: too many children and local dispute with political institutions were listed by the respondents under social causes.

(iii) Personal Causes

Human beings like to lead a trouble free and comfortable life. Along with this the luxurious made of life is also preferred by many. In order to enjoy all the luxuries of life, few women were driven to unlawful activities. This is one of the important personal causes for criminal activity, given by 48 respondents. Economic pursuits in life lead to a craving for more money. This turns into a greedy passion on the longer run. Thus, the greed and impatience to earn more money influence individuals to opt for criminal ways to earn money quickly. This was given as one of the reasons by 42 respondents. Human emotions play a vital role in the day to day life. The emotional status of mind often influence the action of the individual. At times they change the behaviour of the individual radically. In the study also it was cited as the cause for the criminal behaviour of 17 respondents. For self defence, 9 respondents committed crime. Other reasons given were for survival, children's welfare, conflict with daughter and vengeance.

(iv) Illtreatment

Illtreatment of the women in the family assumes many forms and is perpetrated by many individuals. Many respondents reported that they were illtreated by their husbands, in-laws, and other relatives. The various forms of illtreatment faced by the respondents were beating, scolding, made to starve, not allowed to meet the husband and even tried for murder, which might have contributed to the development of criminal attitude among the respondents.

In the present study, illtreatment by husbands (5), illtreatment by relatives (6) and illtreatment by employers (2) were reported as the contributory causes by the respondents. More over the bad habits of the husbands in one way or the other motivated the respondents to behave deviantly.

(v) Illegitimacy

Illegitimate contact of one of the partners in marriage, leads to emotional rift and conflict in the family life. It leads to misunderstandings, and disintegration of conjugal life: ultimately results in criminal activity of the spouse. Illegal contact of the husbands of 17 respondents made them to commit crime. Where as 11 other respondents gave their own illegitimate contact as the reason for committing the criminal act. Illegitimate contact of the dear and near ones (3) forced the respondents involving in criminal behaviour.

Particulars of Acceptance and False Implication

It was reported in various studies that the women criminals have not actually done the crime and admitted that they were falsely implicated by various agencies. It was observed that there was a difference found between the court judgments, motives etc., to the verdict given by the respondents to the researchers. The following analysis convey the details about the acceptance and false implication done as reported by the respondents.

Acceptance

When the respondents were questioned, about their acceptance of their criminal act, half of the respondents (50.40%) accepted the responsibility for the offence. Nearly another half (48.80%) of the respondents did not accept any responsibility for the criminal deed.

TABLE 6.4

Acceptance and False Implication Details

Items	*Frequency*	*Percentage*
Acceptance		
Accepting the crime	63	50.40
Not accepting the crime	61	48.80
No response	01	00.80
False Implication		
Falsely Implicated	44	35.20
Not Falsely Implicated	75	60.00
Do not know	06	04.80
False Implication Done By		
Relatives	07	15.91
Neighbours	13	29.55
Police	10	22.73
Neighbour & Police	03	06.82
Relatives & Police	03	06.82
Others	04*	09.09
Do not know	04	09.09
Total	**44**	**100.20**

* It includes husband-1; son-1; anti-social element-1 and husband and police-1.

False Implication

Three-fifths (60.00%) of the respondents felt that they were not falsely implication in the crime, where as a little more than one third (35.20%) of the respondents maintained that they falsely implicated.

Who Falsely Implicated

Out of the 44 respondents, who felt that they were falsely implicated in the crime, 13 respondents (29.55%) expressed that their neighbours have falsely implicated. Police have implicated 22.73 per cent of then falsely. Relatives have falsely implicated 7 respondents (15.91%). For 7 other respondents, the police along with their husband (1), Relatives (3) and neighbours (3), combined and falsely implicated them. Respondents implicated by husband (1), son (1) or by antisocial elements (1) were also seen. The remaining 4 respondents did not know who implicated them in the crime.

Reasons for False Implication

The various reasons reported by the respondents for such false implications were dispute on property, land and financial matters, illegitimate relations of husbands, respondents and other relatives, local politics, vengeance and purposely misguided by the police.

District-wise Distribution of Respondents

To understand how the respondents were distributed in various districts of Tamil Nadu the following distribution has been made.

TABLE 6.5

District-wise Distribution of Respondents

District	*Frequency*	*Percentage*
Chengalpattu	10	08.00
Cuddalore Valialar	05	04.00
North Arcot Ambedkar	12	09.60
Dharmapuri	02	01.60
Salem	18	14.40
Erode Periyar	04	03.20
The Nilgiris	01	00.80
Trichy	09	07.20
Dindigul Anna	06	04.80
Madurai	28	22.40
Ramnad	05	04.00
Nellai Kattabomman	14	11.20
Kanyakumari	04	03.20
Tuticorin	02	01.60
Other than Tamil Nadu	05	04.00
Total	**125**	**100.00**

The native districts of the respondents were elucidated from the data and it reveals a clear picture. Out of the total 125 respondents 28 respondents (22.40%) were from Madurai district. It is followed by (18 respondents i.e. 14.40%) Salem district. Nellai district has 14 respondents (11.20%). There were 9.60 per cent of respondents from North Arcot district; 8.00 per cent in Chengalpattu district; 7.20 per cent in Trichy and 4.80 per cent in Dindigul Anna district. Each 5 respondents were from Cuddalore Vallalar district as well as from other places outside Tamil Nadu. There were 5 respondents represented Ramnad district in the study sample. Each 4 respondents from Erode Periyar and Kanyakumari district. There were 2 respondents (1.60%) each from Dharmpuri and Tuticorin district and a single respondents from The Nilgiris district.

Time Since the Crime was Committed

The table 6.6 shows the detail of Time when the crime was done by the respondents. For the purpose of calculation the period is calculated in months. Here the period implies the time between the crime done and the study conducted.

TABLE 6.6

Time Since the Crime was Committed

Months	*Frequency*	*Percentage*
Upto 12 months	38	30.40
13 to 24 months	25	20.00
25 to 36 months	12	09.60
37 to 48 months	10	08.00
49 to 60 months	06	04.80
Above 60 months	34	27.20
Total	**125**	**100.00**

The respondents were enquired about the time interval between actual crime and the period when the research work was done, from the responses, the following details came out. Nearly one third (30.40%) of the respondents had committed the crime very recently i.e. within one year. A little more than one fourth (27.20%) of the respondents had committed the crime, before five years.

One fifth (20.00%) of the respondens had done the criminal act before one to two years. One fifth (20.00%) of the respondents had done the criminal act before one to two years. It is concluded that major proportion of respondents committed crime very recently.

Age When Crime was Committed

Age is one of the important factors in criminological literature. Various studies reported that the percentage of young women in the criminal activities is more. This fining is supported in this present study also, however a significant proportion of respondents found in the age group of above 40 years is a notable feature.

TABLE 6.7

Age When Crime was Committed

Age when crime was committed	*Frequency*	*Percentage*
Below 25 years	44	35.20
26 to 30 years	26	20.80
31 to 35 years	15	12.00
36 to 40 years	11	08.80
Above 40 years	29	23.20
Total	125	100.00
Mean	32.42	
S.D.	11.63	

An attempt has been made to find out the age of the respondents when the crime was committed and it revealed the following details. A little more than one third (35.20%) of the respondents had committed the offence when they were below 25 years in age. Nearly one fourth (23.20%) of the respondents were above 40 years in age when they committed the crime or when they committed the criminal act. One fifth of the respondents (20.80%) had done the crime when they were 26-30 years old. The rest of the respondents (12.00% and 8.80%) had committed the criminal deed when they were 31 to 35 years old and 36 to 40 years in age respectively. The mean age in which the crime had been committed was 32.42 years and standard deviation is 11.63 years. It is inferred that the involvement in crime among middle aged women is on the increase.

III. DETAILS OF CRIMES RELATING TO MURDER

Among the crimes, murder is considered more serious since it is an act of killing a human by another human. Murder can be defined as an unlawful act of killing a person with the intention of causing such bodily injury as is likely to cause death or with the knowledge that he/she is likely by such act to cause death. For the purpose of the study the crimes like attempt murder and culpable homicide are clubbed together and categorised in broad heading as crimes relating to murder.

Many of the murder cases result from social interaction of the persons involved in the sense both victim and the criminal may know each other. When conflict grows between either one of them or both or in combination with more than one person; resulting in violence there by causing death due to the emotional imbalance of any one of them. In some cases the murder has already planned so as to decided the act mode of killing, place of killing, etc. In most of the studies it is reported that in majority of the victim involved in crimes the victim is already known to the criminals. All the cases reported in various studies, as far as women crime is concerned the victim is the relative or person known to the criminal. Hence probing into it further gave the numerous facts.

Among the distribution the respondents committed murder found a predominated place and hence in the following pages the details of murder related crimes are presented.

Relationship to the Victim

Researchers in abroad and in India revealed that the offender-victim relationship is high as far as women crime is concerned. The victim includes close relatives, husband, close friends and known persons. Studies by Wolfgang (1958), Mulvihill *et al.* (1969) and in India Ahuja (1970, Rani (1978) revealed that close association of the victim to the criminals were found as far as murder related crimes were concerned. In Ahuja's (1970) study it was observed that more than 50 per cent victim were husbands and 31.5 per cent were close relatives. Study conducted by Sharma (1976) in Punjab revealed that majority of them were close relatives and Rani (1983) in her study conducted in Andhra Pradesh contended that 78.6 per cent of the victim were members of the respondents' family of procreation. Hence in the present study an attempt has been made in the following pages to understand the offender-victim relationship.

TABLE 6.8

Relationship of the Victim

Relationship of the victim	*Frequency*	*Percentage*
Own son, daughter & grand daughter	11	20.00
Husband	07	12.73
Husbands relatives	07	12.73
Other relatives	09	16.36
Husband illegal partner	02	03.63
Dear and near ones' illegal partner	05	09.09
Neighbours	04	07.27
Outsider and unknown person	10	18.18
Total	**55**	**100.00**

There were 56 respondents who had committed crimes relating to murder. For the purpose of classification one respondent who attempted to commit suicide was also included under the same heading, since it involves taking away a human life.

Various studies conducted in the field revealed that in most of the cases the victims were close relatives or persons known to the respondents. In the present study, it was observed that twenty per cent of the respondents murdered their own son, daughter and grand daughter for various reasons. In number of cases the victims were husbands (12.73%) and other relatives (16.36%).

The illegitimacy of their husbands and dear and near ones in one way or other motivated the respondents (09.09%) to murder the illegal partners of their husbands and dear and near ones. It is strange to note that in 18.18 per cent cases the victims were outsiders and persons not known to them. It is to be reported here that the local political quarrels, property dispute etc., have been identified as the causes for the respondents who committed crimes against outsiders and persons unknown to them.

It is inferred that the findings supported various other studies that the victims were close relatives or persons known to respondents. However a notable proportion (18.18%) of the victims were outsiders and persons unknown to respondents.

Accomplice

It is a known fact that women seek the help and assistance to commit crimes. Sometimes they may also extend their help to others in committing a crime. In specific crimes which require physical strength women may seek the assistance and that too from their close relatives or friends. This has been analysed in table 6.9.

Role of the Respondent

To understand the extent of crime among women the role played by the respondents in committing crime is to be taken into consideration. In certain crimes women play the main role and in certain only a subsidiary role. The following table clearly indicates the distribution according to their role in the crime.

TABLE 6.9

Accomplice and Role in Murder Related Crimes

Details	*Frequency*	*Percentage*
Alone or with Accomplice		
Done alone	33	58.93
With accomplice	23	41.07
Total	**56**	**100.00**
Role in the Crime		
Main role	41	73.21
Subsidiary role	15	26.79
Total	**56**	**100.00**

It is observed from the above table that majority of the respondents (73.21%) played the main role in committing the crime implies that nowadays the females are more aggressive and tough as equalled with the male in committing the crime. Seeking and taking assistance from others for criminal activities is common. In the present study also it was noted that in majority of the cases (58.93%) the crimes relating to murder were done alone by the respondents explained their increasing predominant role in the crime.

Nowadays women are also the most able criminals since their main role played in committing crime has increased. They could be equal to men as far as the crime as concerned. They are the equal participants in all the major crimes. Many

Indian studies on the women murderers (Ahuja, 1969; 1970; Nagla, 1991; Rani, 1981; Srivastava, 1975) observed that most of the women murderers were not to be managers, planners or the leaders of crime with which they involve.

TABLE 6.10

Relationship of the Accomplice

Relationship of the Accomplice	*Frequency*	*Percentage*
Husband	5	21.74
Brother	1	04.35
In-law	1	04.35
Friend	2	08.70
Son	2	08.70
Colleague	1	04.35
Illegal husband	2	08.70
Others	9*	39.13
Total	**23**	**100.00**

* Includes Brother & in-law-2; Husband & Friend-1; Husband, In-law & Friend-1; Husband & in-law-1; Husband & son-1; In-law & Friend-1 and Mother-in-law-1.

The above table clearly illustrates the accomplice used by the respondents for committing crimes relating to murder. Most of the respondents as observed in the table seek the help of the close relatives and friends for executing the crime if it involves physical strength and toughness. Moreover the respondents also acted as accomplices in some cases. Majority of the respondents' close relatives acted as accomplices in the present study implies that in order to maintain secrecy and to execute the act perfectly the assistance of the close relatives was required.

Weapon used

Further analysis revealed that various weapons were used by the respondents to kill others. The table presented indicates the details of the weapon used by the respondents. Pollak (1951) contended that women commit felonious crimes mostly by using poisons rather than by using violent methods.

TABLE 6.11

Weapon used

Weapon used	*Frequency*	*Percentage*
Sharp edged weapon	26	47.27
Weapons like crowbar stick rope and stone	11	20.00
Using hand	02	03.64
Burning by kerosene	02	03.64
Pushing into the well	07	12.73
Poisoning	04	07.27
Not accepted as crime done	03	05.45
Total	**55**	**100.00**

A considerable proportion of the respondents (47.27%) who committed crimes relating to murder had used sharp edged weapons for their criminal activity. The use of other weapons like stick, stone, rope, poisoning, burning by kerosene, pushing into the well were used by the respondents as a means to commit their crime.

Details of Non-Murder

The respondents belong to non-murder category comprises 35.20 per cent in the total sample. With a view to have a clear understanding as that of respondents belong to murder category, the details regarding non-murder offenders were collected and presented below. The following table shows the distribution of respondents in various crimes relating to non-murder.

In the non-murder category the highest percentage goes to the trading of illicit liquor (34.78%) followed by prostitution

(28.99%); drug related crimes (20.83%), theft cases (07.25%), quarrelling (04.35%), child kidnapping, Gold Smuggling and sandalwood smuggling each 01.45 per cent. These types of crimes shows that women nowadays engaged in variety of crimes. Though some of the crimes directly affect the victim they may indirectly affect the people and the Government.

TABLE 6.12

Distribution of Crimes Relating to Non-Murder

Nature of Crimes	*Frequency*	*Percentage*
Illicit distillation	24	34.78
Immoral offence	20	28.99
Drug related crimes	14	20.28
Theft related crimes	05	07.25
Others	6*	08.70
Total	**69**	**100.00**

* Includes quarrelling-3; child kidnapping, gold smuggling and sandalwood smuggling each 1.

In this sense the respondents were asked whether they feel that they have done harm to the people or to the Government by committing such crimes.

There were 18 and 20 respondents who felt that they have done harm to the people and Government respectively. It was another 27 and 30 respondents who reiterated that they have not done any harm to the people and Government respectively. More over it is strange to note that there were 24 respondents (35.82%) who justified their criminal act and expressed that they have done 'favour to the people' in the sense that they have done clientele service to the people. In the same context there were 14.93 per cent respondents justified that they by doing their criminal act they generate an additional income to the police and judicial officials by providing them bribe.

Frequency of Crime Done

Unlike crime relating to murder the respondents involved in non-murder crimes were involved in more than once in their criminal activity. Hence the frequency of the crime committed was worked out.

The data collected from the respondents revealed that, 21 respondents (34.43%) have done offences upto 10 times. Of this one-third of them involved in drug related crimes. Among those who committed crimes for 26 to 50 times, fifty per cent belong to illicit distillation comprises two third proportion. For comparative analysis the frequency of crime committed of those who committed crime upto 25 times and the high includes who committed crime above 25 times.

TABLE 6.13

Frequency and Nature of Crime Committed

Nature of crime	*Frequency*			
	Low (upto 25 times)	*High (Above 25 times)*	*Mean frequency*	*Std. Devia*
Illicit distillation	04	20	58.13	23.00
Immorality	09	11	42.10	29.00
Drug related crimes other crimes	21	04	17.75	23.69
Total	**34**	**35**	**21.99**	**30.46**

* Includes drug related crimes-14; theft-5; quarrelling-3; child kidnapping, gold smuggling and sandalwood smuggling each 1.

It is observed from the table that the drug related crimes and other crimes comprises majority in low frequency category and illicit distillation comprises majority in high frequency category implies that the respondents who committed crimes relating to non-murder, mostly were habitual offenders. The mean frequency of illicit distillation is also worked out as 58.13 inferred that the highest frequency of crime done was in illicit distillation.

Role of Accomplice

The role of accomplice or getting or giving assistance in criminal activities is seen in almost all types of crimes. In crimes relating to non-murder category also the role of the accomplice was enquired.

TABLE 6.14

Role and Acomplice in Crime Relating to Non-Murder

Details	*Frequency*	*Percentage*
Alone or with accomplice		
Done alone	29	42.03
With accomplice	40	57.94
Total	**69**	**100.00**
Role in the crime		
Main role	51	73.91
Subsidiary role	18	26.09
Total	**69**	**100.00**
Relation of accomplice		
Husband	13	32.50
Relatives	10	25.00
Friend & Colleague	11	27.50
Illegal Husband	02	05.00
Do not know	04	10.00
Total	**40**	**100.00**

It is observed that more than half of the respondents (57.94%) committed crimes with accomplice in the sense that they give and take assistance for their criminal activities. There were 42.03 per cent respondents who committed the crime all alone. When enquired about the relationship of the accomplice to the respondents it is revealed that they shows the distribution of the relationship of the accomplice with the respondents.

It was observed that the accomplice were invariably known to the respondents. In many cases the accomplice is a close relative or friend. In 13 cases the husbands (36.11%) of the respondents were the accomplice. In 11 cases the accomplice (28.56%) were friends and colleagues. In 10 cases the accomplice were close relatives other than their husbands. In four cases the respondents were not aware who smuggling and prostitution. In such cases at every stage the organiser maintain secrecy of accomplice at different stages. Naturally all the persons involving in the chain may not be aware of the other links.

It is inferred that in crimes relating to murder the majority of the accomplice were from close relatives, but as far as the crimes relating non-murder category is concerned a considerable proportion of the accomplice belong to friends and colleagues. Since many crimes under this category needs network and assistance. And it is not also an one day affair.

It is further revealed that in our study, majority of the respondents (68.11%) played the main role in executing the crime.

General Information Regarding Arrest Particulars

Many a time the person who committed crime tried to escape from the law for the fear of punishment. For some their conscience or other factors motivate them to surrender themselves before the court of law. Hence an attempt has been made to understand the behaviour of the respondents on these issues.

TABLE 6.15

Information Regarding Surrender and Arrest

Arrest and Surrender Particulars	*Frequency*	*Percentage*
Trying to escape	**n : 125**	
Tried to escape	33	26.40
Did not try to escape	92*	73.60
Surrender to Police	**n : 125**	
Surrendered to police	13	10.40
Did not surrendered	112*	89.60
Reasons for surrender		
Fear of punishment	01	07.69
Instigation by neighbours	01	07.69
Conscience	08	61.55
Advice by relatives	01	07.69
To get reduced punishment	01	07.69
Others	01	07.69

* Cases includes those who had not accepted their crime and false implicated cases (as reported by the respondents).

People react differently to the situation immediately after they commit crime in this study when enquired the respondents gave following details, a little more than one fourth (26.40%) of the respondents tried to escape after they committed crime.

The remaining 92 respondents (73.6%) did not try to escape. Only 13 respondents (10.4%) surrendered to the police immediately after the committed crime. The majority of the respondents did not surrender to the police.

Among the 13 respondents who surrendered to the police, 8 respondents did so because of their conscience. The remaining 5 respondents surrendered because of fear of more punishment (1), instigation by neighbour (1), advice of relative (1), to get reduce punishment (1) and the combination of all these reasons (1).

7

Consequences on Individual, Children, Family and Society

The impact of the criminal behaviour and its aftermath have considerable consequences on the individual, family and society at large. The disgrace and the stigma attached to the criminal behaviour cause (in the individual) a considerable deterioration of his/her self esteem and personality. In order to have an understanding about the consequences an individual supposed to face due to their criminal act, the respondents were enquired. A structured interview schedule has been used for the purpose. The consequences are broadly classified into four areas, viz., consequences on individual, consequences on children, consequences on family and consequences on society. In each area ten important factors were identified and listed. It is important to note that these identified factors do not necessarily have any impact directly on the respondents due to their criminal behaviour. It is the question of how they felt and/or experienced in broad areas as statements and measured using a Likert type 5-point scale as explained below.

Score :	5	4	3	2	1
Scale :	Fully Agree	Agree	Neutral	Disagree	Fully Disagree

All the statements were measured using the above score.

A. On the Individual

To estimate how far the individual's education, occupation, financial life, personal, psychological and familial life along with social participation, are affected due to the criminal behaviour, the following analysis has been made.

TABLE 7.1

Consequences of the Individual

Statements	*Fully Agree*	*Agree*	*Neutral*	*Disagree*	*Fully Disagree*	*Mean Score*
	(5)	(4)	(3)	(2)	(1)	
Due to crime academic life is affected	65	25	12	07	16	3.92
Crime involves financial loss	68	25	06	07	19	3.92
Social status has been affected	86	24	04	03	08	4.42
Personal life has been affected	96	17	02	05	05	4.55
Individual freedom is affected	96	17	02	06	04	4.56
Criminals feel depressed affected	91	18	05	06	05	4.47
Criminals feel detached from the family	86	25	05	02	07	4.45
Criminals feel sense of guilt	78	30	06	07	04	4.37
Criminals often get self anger	76	21	07	09	12	4.12
Criminals feel detached from the entire society	83	23	05	03	11	4.31
Total	**825**	**225**	**54**	**55**	**91**	**43.10**

It is observed from the table 7.1. that half of the respondents fully agreed that the academic life is affected due to crime. One fifth of the respondents agreed to this contention. The mean score worked out is 3.92. A little more than half of the respondents admitted strongly that crime creates financial loss and one fifth of the respondents agreed with this admission and they rated the mean score for this statements as 3.92.

A little above two thirds of the respondents felt that social status of a persons gets affected as observed in the table. Three fourth of the respondents fully agreed that crime affects personal life and also a little above one tenth of the respondents agreed to this.

More than seventy per cent of the respondents felt that the individual freedom is affected due to crime. A little more than one tenth of the respondents have agreed to this feeling. A major portion of 72.80 percentage of the respondents agreed fully that criminals feel depressed. A shade above one tenth of the respondents agreed with this notion.

As the mean worked out as 4.45, nearly two third of the respondents agreed strongly that criminals detached from their family and one fifth of the respondents also agreed to this statement. A little less than two third of the respondents agreed fully that individuals have a sense of guilt, because of their criminal act. Nearly one fourth of the respondents agreed and endorse this view.

Three fifths of the respondents were of the strong opinion that criminals are often self depreciating and get angered towards themselves. The mean score rated for this statement is 4.12. Major proportion of the respondents agreed that individuals who had committed crime, feel detached from the entire society and the mean score is worked out as 4.31.

It is inferred that the respondents' perceived the consequences on the individual level as high. When looked at the mean score for each factors it is seen that all the respondents have agreed to the statements. The mean score ranged from 3.92 to 4.56 which implied that majority of the respondents felt and/or experienced the consequences of crime at the individual level.

B. On the Children

The respondents were asked to rate the consequence of crime on the children, invariably whether they are married or unmarried or having children or not.

TABLE 7.2

Consequences on the Children

Statements	*Fully Agree*	*Agree*	*Neu-tral*	*Dis-agree*	*Fully Dis-agree*	*Mean Score*
	(5)	(4)	(3)	(2)	(1)	
Children's upbringing is a problem.	75	38	06	02	04	4.42
Irreparable loss to the children.	85	28	05	07	00	4.53
Children's education is a problem.	92	16	07	04	06	4.47
Children's personality affected.	49	40	14	08	14	3.82
Children loss moral support.	68	36	04	09	08	4.18
A negative model to the children.	74	24	08	08	11	4.14
Loss control over children	62	29	18	07	09	4.02
Children face social harassment.	67	29	07	07	15	4.00
Children may be exposed to criminal.	75	29	08	07	06	4.28
Mother is the most important factor in upbringing children.	96	23	02	03	01	4.68
Total	**743**	**294**	**79**	**62**	**74**	**42.54**

It is observed from the table that the mean score is estimated to low range of 3.82 to high range of 4.68. All the respondents agreed to each statement, which implied that the crime final activity of the parents will have a greater adverse consequence on the upbringing (4.42 mean score), education (mean score 4.47), personality (mean score 3.82) and moral support mean score 4.18) of their children. It was agreed by the respondents that parents criminal activities result in irreparable loss to the children (4.53). Major proportion (4.40) of the respondents also agreed that when they indulge in crime they become a negative model to their children which in turn influence the children to behave deviantly. Moreover, they may loss their control over the children (mean score 4.02) also.

When the parents indulge in criminal activities, the children at many circumstances, get exposed to criminal risk and also face social harassment from other members of the society. This contention is very well supported by the respondents when they rated the statement with the mean score of 4.00 for social harassment and 4.28 for exposure to criminal risk.

Mother is the basic unit of the family where is she has to socialize the children in such a way that they should be a normal being of the community. The role of the mother in each and every family is most significant and crucial in upbringing the children. The respondents also strongly agreed (mean score 4.68) that mother is the important factors in upbringing the children and her place cannot be substituted by any one else.

C. On the Family

Family is the basic unit of the society, where in each member has an influential role to perform in the sense that both the individual and the family influence each other. When one member in the family and its member. With a view to analyse how far the family gets affected either due to one or more deviant members, the following analysis with ten statement was made. The respondents were asked to rate these statements.

TABLE 7.3

Consequence on the Family

Statements	*Fully Agree*	*Agree*	*Neu-tral*	*Dis-agree*	*Fully Dis-agree*	*Mean Score*
	(5)	(4)	(3)	(2)	(1)	
Parent (in law) feel mental agony.	77	18	07	10	13	4.09
Economic loss to the family.	66	21	08	09	21	3.82
Family face social harassment	69	23	04	09	20	3.90
Status of the family affected	81	21	06	06	11	4.24
As a negative model to siblings.	71	23	12	08	11	4.08
Irreparable loss to the husband/parents.	61	22	18	07	17	3.82
Marriage/marital life is a problem.	64	18	16	11	16	3.82
Siblings future life affected.	71	18	06	17	13	3.94
Neighbour's relationship affected.	77	23	06	09	10	4.18
Leads to disintegration of family.	98	15	04	07	01	4.62
Total	**735**	**202**	**67**	**93**	**133**	**40.50**

It is revealed from the table 7.3 that the respondents rated not only the parents or parents-in-law feel mental agency (mean score 4.09) but also the siblings whose future life (mean score 3.94) gets affected due to the criminal behaviour. The mean score of 3.90 and 4.24 have been rated by the respondents when they felt that the family face social harassment and the status of the family is affected respectively.

The financial loss accounted for majority of the respondents (mean score 3.82) when they rated the consequences of the crime on the family. With regard to marriage, respondents felt that due to criminal behaviour the marriage is itself a problem, if the person is unmarried; and marital life becomes trouble, if the person is married (mean score 3.82).

Previous studies revealed that the husband is one of the important persons whose life is worsely affected when his partner is involved in criminal activity and subsequent imprisonment. On the part of the husband some sexual adjustments is also needed. If the individual is unmarried, then it becomes an irreparable loss to the parents. The above contention was very supported by the respondents and the mean score is rated as 3.82.

Not only every individual and family have adverse consequences, but also the neighbours' relationships with the deviant family which gets deteriorated as agreed by many respondents (mean score 4.18).

It is contended that the deviant behaviour ultimately results in family disintegration (4.62) and the highest mean score has been assigned by the study sample to this statement, as far as the consequences of crime on the family is concerned. As revealed in various studies that the female criminality have disastrous consequences on the social structure the results reported by the respondents emphasised the point seriously.

D. On the Society

The consequences of criminal behaviour is not on the individual, children and family but also on the society at large where the respondents is the member. Hence at large where the criminal behaviour affects the society in terms of finance, religious, social and political participation etc., were analysed in the following table.

TABLE 7.4

Consequences on the Soceity

Statements	*Fully Agree*	*Agree*	*Neu-tral*	*Dis-agree*	*Fully Dis-agree*	*Mean Score*
	(5)	(4)	(3)	(2)	(1)	
Criminals feel that they have done much harm to the community.	39	33	10	17	26	3.34
Criminals feel that their activity has done harm to the Government.	33	25	19	19	29	3.11
Criminals understand that their crime resulted in loss to the Government.	32	22	25	11	35	3.04
Resulted in Law and order problem	21	12	35	23	34	2.70
Participation in social activities is lessened due to criminal acts.	44	35	16	14	16	3.62
Criminal behaviour influences the neighbour negatively.	50	29	19	16	11	3.73
Criminal behaviour lessens political participation.	28	19	33	19	26	3.03
Criminal behaviour lessens religious participation.	43	28	20	13	21	3.47
Criminals sow seeds to problematic society.	56	30	11	18	10	3.83
The society gets polluted due to criminal activities.	62	24	18	13	26	3.83
Total	**408**	**257**	**206**	**163**	**216**	**33.82**

The respondents felt and rated that the criminal activity results in harming the community in one way or the other with a mean score of 3.34. The deviant behaviour causes a considerable harm, financial loss to the Government in ways of police, judicial and prison expenses. In crimes like illicit distillation, tax evading, theft, sandalwood smuggling etc., a considerable loss to the Government is incurred. The respondents were also of them of the same opinion that the criminal activity results in harm (3.11), and financial loss (3.04) to the Government. The respondents agreed that their activity lessens social participation (3.62), finance participation (3.67)., religious participation (3.47) and political participation (3.03).

The influence of the neighbour has a considerable effect on the individual hence to assess whether the criminal behaviour has any influence on the neighbour, the respondents were asked to report whether the criminal behaviour influence the neighbour negatively. It is noted that even without the influenced. It is agreed that the neighbours were influenced negatively, in other words, the respondents become a negative model to the neighbours (mean score 3.73).

By deviant behaviour a problematic society has been created and ultimately the society gets polluted. These two statements accounted for the mean score of 3.83 and 3.95 respectively.

Conclusion

It is enclosed from the overall analysis that the respondents invariably agreed that a significant consequence of the deviant behaviour can be noticed on individual level (Total mean score 43.10), children's level (Total mean score 42.54), family level (Total mean score 40.56) and on the society at large (Total mean score 33.82).

It is strange to note that though major proportion of the respondents were aware that their criminal behaviour has a considerable consequence on the social structure, some of them would like to indulge in crime in future, suggests that urgent remedial steps have to be taken to prevent these women from involving in crime any more.

8
Prison Life and Future Plan

Prison Life

Imprisonment is one of the methods used to handle the convicts in such a way to protect and prevent them to commit further crimes for a specific period of time and also to prevent others from committing crime on them out of vengeance. The concept of punishing the criminals by imprisonment has recently been changed to treatment and rehabilitation with a view to modify the criminal tendencies among them. Scholars in the correctional work nowadays are more concerned about the facilities provided in the prison, educational and vocational training and the social organisation within the prison so as to examine the adequacy of such facilities in fulfilling the objectives of rehabilitation and reformation. As far as the condition in the Indian prison is concerned they are grossly inadequate. There are only few prisons specially meant for women in each State and in many places women prisons form part of the male prison. The Committee on the Status of Women in India (1974) reported that women prisoners live in a pathetic condition. These prison are normally overcrowded, and with lack of educational, vocational and welfare facilities. Instead of treating them for rehabilitation these prisons are only isolating and separating the females from the community where they lived. Hence in this chapter attempts have been made to understand the satisfaction level of the welfare services provided in the prison, particulars regarding visits made by relatives, impact of prison life, problems faced and suggestions for improvement.

Facilities Available in the Prison

The respondents were enquired about their satisfaction level of the various welfare facilities provided to them in the prison. A five point scale has been used to quantity their level of satisfaction. The scores assigned are 5-Highly satisfied: 4-satisfied: 3-Neutral: 2-Dissatisfied and 1-Highly dissatisfied.

As various studies revealed, the welfare facilities available in these prisons were not satisfactory. They are grossly ineffective and inefficient. The mean score of these facilities ranges from 1.22 to 2.34. Among the food provided the break-fast and dinner have been rated by the respondents as low: in total the food is not at the satisfactory level. Moreover, the mean score for both work and incentives available in the prison, were reported as dissatisfactory. Facilities regarding accommodation, bathing, clothing, medical facilities and recreational facilities have been rated as in the mean score of 2.24, 2.23, 1.94, 2.2 and .85 respectively. When enquired about the educational and vocational training, the respondents expressed dissatisfaction and the mean scores are also worked out as 1.34 and 1.35 respectively.

Prison is considered as a social system wherein a prisoner has to live with other inmates whether she likes or not and hence the co-inmates have a considerable role to play in influencing the behaviour and personality of the individual. It is observed from the table that the relationship of the fellow inmates with respondents were a little above dissatisfaction level. The mean score is 2.34.

TABLE 8.1

Level of Satisfaction of the Facilities in Prison

Facilities	*Highly Satisfied*	*Satis- fied*	*Neu- tral*	*Dissati- sfied*	*Highly Dissati- sfied*	*Mean Score*
	(5)	(4)	(3)	(2)	(1)	
1. Food						
(i). Break Fast	6	13	0	37	69	1.80
(ii). Lunch	7	13	1	34	70	1.82
(iii).Dinner	7	12	1	34	71	1.80
2. Accommodation	16	19	3	28	59	2.24
3. Bathing	15	19	5	27	59	2.23
4. Clothing	7	15	7	31	65	1.94
5. Medical Facilities	14	18	6	28	59	2.20
6. Recreational	7	6	9	42	61	1.85
7. Other Welfare Facilities	5	7	11	31	71	1.75
8. Educational Facilities	5	10	4	10	96	1.54
9. Vocational training	2	1	9	15	98	1.35
10. Work/Labour	1	5	7	9	103	1.34
11. Incentives (if any)	2	0	3	13	107	1.22
12. Grievance redressal	5	20	7	46	47	2.12
13. Relationship with Fellow	9	23	19	25	49	2.34
14. Communication Facilities	7	20	12	42	44	2.23
15. Treatment by the Staff	6	25	13	39	42	2.31
Total	**121**	**226**	**117**	**491**	**1170**	**32.10**

Communication is one of the ways in which the prisoner can have contact with the outside world. Which in turn facilitates a feeling of community belongingness, though that has been isolated from the community. Hence it is important to provide such facilities to the prisoner. It has been observed that most of the respondents were not satisfied with the communication facility available in prison (mean score is 2.23).

It is a general opinion that the prison officials instead of treating and rehabilitating the prisoners they illitreate them under the garb of security. It is to be kept in mind that the concept of punishment has been changed to treatment and rehabilitation. Most of them reported dissatisfaction towards the treatment meted out by the prison officials. The mean score is retired by the respondents as 2.31.

As observed from the above discussion that major proportion of the respondents were not satisfied with the facilities provided such as food, accommodation, bathing, clothing, medical, recreation, educational, vocational training, work incentives, grievance redressal, relationship with co-inmates, etc. Hardly few respondents were satisfied with these facilities.

The above result suggests that improvements much be made in providing these facilities so as to make the prison life, highly rehabilitative.

TABLE 8.2

Punishment Period

Punishment Period	*Frequency*	*Percentage*
Upto 3 months	45	36.00
More than 3 months to 1 year	16	12.80
More than 1 year to 5 years	05	04.00
More than 5 years to 10 years	05	04.00
More than 10 years to 14 years	06	04.80
More than 14 years	48	38.40
Total	**125**	**100.00**

Punishment Period

The respondents were distributed in the table 8.2 by their period of imprisonment. The length or sentence is associated with the seriousness of the offence as well.

There were 48 respondents (46.15%) sentenced for more than 14 years. There were also 6 respondents who were sentenced for life. There were each five respondents sentenced to imprisonment for 10 years and 5 years respectively. A considerable proportion of respondents were served a term of 4 months to one year. Little more than one third (36.00%) of them belonged upto 3 months category.

Visits Made by Relative and Friends

Visits made by their family members, relatives and friends often make the prisoner to feel that they are not away from the community. The prisoners contact to the non-criminal world is only possible through these visits. This indirectly make the prisoners to feel that they are not isolated and separated from their community. Hence visits made by relatives and friends and exchange of letter correspondence have been permitted with certain restrictions. There is a specified time and date for such visits made under the guard of prison personnel.

Little more than half of the respondents (52.80%) had visitors. For 11.20 per cent of the respondents, since their sentence started very recently, had no visitors. The various reasons enumerated for no visitors are travel expenses, stigma attached due to their criminal act and to maintain secrecy. It is inferred that these respondents who had no contact with the outside world may face problems after release and it may hinder the rehabilitation process as well.

TABLE 8.3

Visits by Relatives and Friends

Visits By Relatives/Friends	*Frequency*	*Percentage*
Visits by relatives		
Relatives/friends visiting the respondent	67	53.60
No visitors	44	35.20
Not applicable	14*	11.20
Frequency of visits		
Once in 15 months	14	20.90
Once in a month	15	22.39
Once in two months	02	02.99
Once in three months	09	13.43
Once in six months	12	17.91
Once in a year	10	14.93
Once in two years	02	02.99
Rare visits (above two years)	03	04.48
Total	**67****	**100.00**

* Very recently admitted in the prison

** 14 respondents who were very recently admitted in the prison and 44 respondents who had no visitors.

Time Between Visites

Among those respondents who had visitors, a good number of respondents (22.39%) had visitors every month and also considerable proportion of respondents (20.90%) had visitors once in 15 days which made them feel that they were not isolated from the community. There were 17.91 per cent of respondents whose visitors visited them once in six months. When these visits were made it is easy for the rehabilitation process to facilitate its course.

Impact of Prison Life

In order to assess the impact of the prison life the

respondents were asked whether it helped or harmed them. More over whether their personality has been improved or not was also enquired.

It was observed that 40.80 per cent of the respondents felt that the prison life in one way or the other helped them and for other 20.00 per cent regard the prison life it had not helpful in any way. A considerable percentage (36.20%) were not in a position to judge whether it helped them or not. It is also to be kept in mind that 12.80 per cent of the respondents were admitted in the prison very recently.

When enquired about whether the prison life had done any harm, 15.20 per cent of respondents reiterated that the prison had done harm to these respondents instead of helping them to overcome their problems. The ways in which the prison had harmed were listed in a separate table.

There were 45 respondents (36.00%) who admitted that their personality had been improved due to the prison life. A considerable proportion of the respondents (24.00%) admitted that their personality has not been improved. The remaining 40.00 per cent of them did not know whether their personality has been improved or not.

Prison Life ways Hilped and Harmed

To understand the impact of prison life on the respondents further probe into the ways in which the respondents were helped or harmed are done in the proceeding analysis.

Among those who reported that the prison life had helped them, majority of them (74.51%) expressed that it helped to change their bad character and criminal attitude. The other respondents who reported that the prison life had given them a chance to correct themselves, change bad character and to understand family responsibility.

TABLE 8.4

Helpful Effect of Prison Life

Sl.No.	*Helpful Effect*	*Frequency*	*Percentage*
1.	To change bad character	02	03.92
2.	A chance to correct oneself	05	09.80
3.	To understand family responsibility	02	03.92
4.	Sl.No. 1 and Sl.No.3	38	74.51
5.	Sl.No. 1 and Sl.No.3 and vocational training	04	06.84
	Total	**51**	**100.00**

TABLE 8.5

Helpful Effect of Prison Life

Sl.No.	*Helpful Effect*	*Frequency*	*Percentage*
1.	Punishment oriented & not rehabilitation oriented	01	05.26
2.	Prison environment is harmful	04	21.04
3.	Not allowed to correct one self and chances to increase criminal tendency.	01	05.26
4.	S.No. 1, & S.No. 2	07	36.84
5.	S.No. 1, S.No. 2, & S.No.3	02	10.52
	Total	**19**	**100.00**

Though prison life helped some of the respondents it also had a negative impact on them. There were 19 respondents who felt that the prison life harmed them, reported that the prison life is more of punishment oriented and not rehabilitation oriented and the environment is also harmful. Few of them also felt that the chances to correct oneself is lesser than the chances available to develop criminal tendencies.

Prison Environment and Relationship with Coinmates

To overcome the deprivations resulting from prison life prisoners associate themselves with co-inmates for mutual help and protection. To sustain a feeling of solidarity among them they establish certain norms, values and relationship pattern among inmates. Some times these associations become compulsory since no way is left out howsoever one way like or dislike the co-inmates. The factors of selecting friends depends on caste, nativity, housed in one barracks, same age group and similar habits were identified as important factors in such selections. It is interesting to note that, relating with persons convicted for crimes like immorality, illicitly distillation and theft is considered awful by other inmates who were imprisoned for other crime.

Problems Faced in the Prison

Various studies and jail committee reported revealed that the women prisoners were in a pathetic condition, housed in an unhygienic accommodation and the facilities available were grossly ineffective. With a view to understand the difficulties faced by the respondents in these prisons in Tamil Nadu, the respondents were enquired about the problems they faced in the prison and the responses are distributed in table 8.6.

Most of the respondents reported that the food served, the cosmetics supplied and the dress given were inadequate and poor in quality. The barracks were over crowding. The vocational training is grossly ineffective which cannot in any way fetch employment after release. It is important to note that the prisoners from Madurai prison have no vocational training or work inside the prison and they all felt that keeping idle is the great problem to them.

TABLE 8.6

Problems Faced by the Respondents in the Prison

Problems Faced	*Frequency**
No quality food dress and cosmetics	110
No Privacy	096
Not taken care	102
No redressal to complaints	063
Lack of recreation and communication facilities	095
Quarrelsome nature of co-inmates	023
Staff harassment	067

* Multiple response

The recreation and communication facilities were not adequate as felt by the respondents. Most of the (120) respondents felt that they were not taken care and their complaints were not redressed properly by the officials. There were 67 respondents also reported that the staff in the prison harass them under the guard of security. Co-inmates were also one of the problems for 23 respondents. The responses were multiple in nature; single respondents reported one or more number of difficulties.

It is concluded that the difficulties faced by the respondents should be adequately dealt with and due consideration should be given to them so as to make themselves satisfied with prison life which could facilities their involvement freely in the rehabilitation programmes.

Suggestions for Improvement

For any successful programme that participation of the people's involvement is crucial. Hence to get the people's participation it is important not only ask them to identify the problem areas but also their suggestions to solve it. In the present study also, the respondents were asked to suggest some of the measures to be taken to make the prison life rehabilitative.

TABLE 8.7

Suggestions by the Respondents

Suggestions by Respondents	*Frequency**
Quality and quantity in food, cosmetics and dress	112
Spacious accommodation	108
Provisions for and/or employment oriented vocational training	113
Educational programmes and guidance	115
Adequate in medical facilities	098
Improvement in medical facilities	076
Provisions for recreational facilities and dress	054
Adequate communication facilities	094
Early redressal, treatment & care	120

* Multiple response.

There were 112 respondents suggested that quality and quantity must be improved in food, cosmetics and dress supplied to them. As far as the accommodation is concerned over crowding should be avoided, since most of the respondents felt that no privacy could be maintained. The respondents who suggested that vocational training education programmes, guidance and incentives should be provided in par with the present day labour market with the outside world and should be in high standards. Adequate recreational (54) and medical facilities (76) were suggested by the respondents. More over the respondents were also reported that improvement the communication facilities (94) and treatment of the staff in a humanitarian way (120) should has given die consideration.

It is concluded that when the above said suggestions were properly dealt with, the prison life could be more of a rehabilitative one than the existing condition.

Future Plan After Release

The effectiveness of prisonization has been understood by future plans of the respondents also. The follow up programmes should be based on the future plan of the respondents so as to make it more effective. The future plan of the respondents also suggest us the ways in which effective rehabilitative programmes could be implemented. With these ideas in mind the following analysis has been made to understand their future plans, where they would like to go, what type of occupations they would engage, whether family and society would accept them, help expected from the government, the problems they would face and assurance of not indulging in crime.

TABLE 8.8

Respondents' Future Plans after Release

Future Plans after Release	*Frequency*	*Percentage*
Proposed Place of Stay	**n : 125**	
To live with husband	41	32.80
To live with their parents	42	33.60
To live with daughter, son, brother and sister	21	16.40
To other relatives	07	05.60
Do not know	14	11.20
Proposed Activities after Release		
Agriculture	14	11.20
Coolie/manual work	27	21.60
Self Employment	30	24.00
Searching for employment	17	13.60
Criminal activities	13	10.40
Do not know	24	19.20

Among the 125 samples studied, each little more than one third of them admitted that they would go to their husbands and parents after release. Among those who would like to live with parents (42), only three of them were unmarried and vast majority of 39 of them were admitted. It is to be understood that these 39 respondents, did not like to live with their husbands or in the family of procreation is congenital. For other 16.40 per cent, they prefer to live with their daughter, son, brother and sister. There were also seven respondents who had plan to live with other relatives.

The respondents were asked what type of occupations or activities they would engage after release and the responses obtained were also listed.

Nearly one fourth of them (24.00%) revealed that they would try for self employment by starting a small business like petty shop, vegetable vending, fruit stall etc. A considerable number of respondents (21.60%) admitted that they would engage themselves as coolie in agricultural and non-agricultural fields for daily wages. There were 17 respondents (11.20%) who felt that they would search for employment. There were 13 respondents (10.40%) reiterated that they would again indulge in criminal activities after release; for them the prison life has no significant role to play or they not changed in their criminal attitude.

Acceptance of Family and Society After Release

Criminality is itself involves social disgrace and social stigma. The situation becomes rather worse if a female is involved in crime since the criminality of women is seriously looked into for the reason that the consequences of criminality of women as compared to men is greater on the social structure. In many cases the convicted women is looked down upon; and husbands and other relatives are reluctant to even visit them in prison due to the fear of social stigma. In such a situation whether the women after release will be acceptable by the family is an interesting question.

TABLE 8.9

Respondents' Perception of Acceptance of Family and Society

Perception	*Frequency*	*Percentage*
I. Family Acceptance		
Family would accept the respondent	70	56.00
Family would not accept	50	40.00
Do not know	05	04.00
II. Society Acceptance		
Society would accept them	27	21.60
Society would not accept	94	75.20
Do not know	04	03.20

It is clear from the above table that 56.00 per cent and 21.60 per cent of the respondents perceive that their family and society should accept them, respectively. There were majority of the respondents (75.20%) admitted that the society would not accept them after release inferred that the respondents had not lost their high values on the society and hence every chances to rehabilitate them is easy.

Family of Acceptance and Nature of Crime Committed

Indepth analysis has been done in the following pages about the perceived acceptance of family and society with the nature of crime committed.

Among the 125 respondents majority of the respondents (56.00%) were very confident that their family would accept them after release; among them both respondents from murder related crimes and non-murder related crimes were equally

TABLE 8.10

Family Acceptance and Nature of Crime Committed

Nature of Crime	*Family acceptance*			*Total*
	Accept	*Do not Accept*	*Do not Know*	
Type I				
Murder	35	18	03	56
	(62.50)	(32.14)	(05.36)	(100.00)
Non-murder	35	32	02	69
	(50.72)	(46.38)	(02.90)	(100.00)
Type II				
Involves victim	35	23	03	61
	(57.38)	(37.70)	(04.92)	(100.00)
Involves no-victim	35	27	02	64
	(54.69)	(42.18)	(03.13)	(100.00)
Type III				
Against person	35	22	03	60
	(58.33)	(36.67)	(05.00)	(100.00)
Against property	29	14	02	45
	(64.44)	(31.11)	(04.44)	(100.00)
Against Morality	06	14	0	20
	(30.00)	(70.00)		(100.00)
Type IV				
Convicts	49	41	04	94
	(52.13)	(43.62)	(04.26)	(100.00)
Undertrials	21	09	01	31
	(67.74)	(29.03)	(03.23)	(100.00)
Type V				
Long termers	34	19	04	57
	(59.65)	(33.33)	(07.02)	(100.00)
Short termers	36	31	01	68
	(52.94)	(45.59)	(01.47)	(100.00)

distributed. A considerable number (50) of respondents (40.00%) admitted that their family would not accept them after release and in that the respondents belonging to non-murder category comprises the majority (64.00%). It was also interesting to note that there were five respondents who did not know whether their family would accept them or not. More or less the same trend has been observed as far as the respondents belonging to crimes involving victim and no-victim are concerned.

Among the 70 respondents who reiterated that their family would accept them after release, fifty per cent were from crimes against person, 41.43 per cent were from crime against property and the rest 8.57 per cent of the respondents from immoral crimes. Among the 50 respondents (40.00%) who confessed that their family would not accept them, 44.00 per cent (22) had committed to crime against property and immorality. Among the 20 respondents who involved in immoral crime, majority of them (14) admitted that their family would not accept them after release. It is inferred that among crimes certain types of crimes were considered as awful by the society. Though all are criminal activities, crimes against property and immorality are considered as awful or bad than crimes against person. Hence in the present study the rate of acceptance of family for the respondents relating to crimes against property and morality is less than the respondents relating to crimes against person.

As far as the convicts and under trials were concerned among those (50) who felt that their family would not accept them after release, majority of 41 respondents (82.00%) were convicts. Among 31 under trials majority of them (67.74%) felt that their family would accept them after release.

When the length of sentence is taken into consideration, among those felt that their family would not accept them (50), majority of 31 respondents (62.00%) were short termers.

Those felt that their family would accept them (34 and 36), were distributed more or less equally among long termers and short termers.

Accetance of Society and Nature of Crime Committed

The respondents were asked whether the society would accept them after release. Since the rehabilitation programme is succeed only when the women prisoners settle down again in the society as a normal human being. Hence the society must be in a position to accept them. When the responses of the respondents were matched with the nature of the crime it gave some interesting results.

Contrary to the acceptance as the family, majority of 94 respondents (75.20%) were of the opinion that the society would not accept them after release. It is also important to note that a considerable number of respondents thought that their family would accept them but the society would not accept them after release.

Among the 69 respondents belong to the non-murder category majority (54) of them felt that the society would not accept them after release. In the case of respondents involved in murder related crimes also the same trend has been observed. It is inferred that there is no significant difference between the opinion of the respondents on non-acceptance of the society as far as murder and non-murder crimes are concerned.

There is no significant difference between the respondents on their three respondenses viz., society would accept them, would not accept them and do not know whether it would accept them or not, as far as crime involving victim and no-victim crime categories are concerned.

With regard to the respondents from immorality (20) eighty five per cent admitted that the society would not accept them. Among the 60 respondents who committed crime against person confessed that the society would not accept them. In the crime against property category there were 45 respondents, among them majority of them (32) reported that the society would not accept them after release.

Among the 94 convicted, majority of (72) the respondents reiterated that the society would not accept them after release. There were 68 short termers and 57 long termers, among them, majority of them (48 and 46 respectively) were of the opinion that they would not be accepted by the society after release. It is concluded that more respondents belong to non-murder, victimless crime, immorality, short termers and convict categories felt that the family and society would not accept them after release than felt by other type of offenders.

TABLE 8.12

Family Accepance and Society Acceptance

Family Acceptance	*Society acceptance*			*Total*
	Accept	*Do not Accept*	*Do not Know*	
Accept	25 (92.59)	44 (46.81)	01 (25.00)	70 (56.00)
Do not accept	02 (07.41)	46 (48.94)	02 (50.00)	50 (40.00)
Do not know	0	04 (04.26)	01 (25.00)	05 (04.00)
Total	**27** **(100.00)**	**94** **(100.00)**	**04** **(100.00)**	**125** **(100.00)**

It was observed that one fifth of the respondents felt that both their family and society would accept them after release. Among those who confessed that the family would accept them (27) after release, vast majority of 92.59 per cent also felt that the society would accept them after release.

TABLE 8.11

Society Acceptance and Nature of Crime

Nature of Crime	*Family acceptance*			*Total*
	Accept	*Do not Accept*	*Do not Know*	
Type I				
Murder	13	43	0	56
	(23.21)	(76.79)		(100.00)
Non-murder	14	51	04	69
	(20.29)	(73.91)	(05.80)	(100.00)
Type II				
Involves victim	14	46	01	61
	(22.96)	(75.41)	(01.64)	(100.00)
Involves no-victim	13	48	03	64
	(20.31)	(75.00)	(04.69)	(100.00)
Type III				
Against person	14	45	01	60
	(23.33)	(75.00)	(04.44)	(100.00)
Against property	11	32	02	45
	(24.44)	(71.11)	(04.44)	(100.00)
Against morality	02	17	01	20
	(10.00)	(85.00)	(05.00)	(100.00)
Type IV				
Convicts	20	72	02	94
	(21.27)	(76.60)	(02.13)	(100.00)
Undertrials	07	22	02	31
	(22.58)	(70.97)	(06.45)	(100.00)
Type V				
Long termers	11	46	0	57
	(19.30)	(80.70)		(100.00)
Short termers	16	48	04	68
	(23.53)	(70.59)	(05.88)	(100.00)

Among those who felt that the family would accept them after release (70), more than fifty per cent felt that family accept them. Those who felt that both the society and family would not accept them constituted a significant number (46) in the study sample of 125 respondents.

Assurance Regarding Involvement in Crime in Future

The respondents were further enquired to give their assurances whether they would indulge in crime in future i.e. after release: with a view to find out the effectiveness of the prisonization on these respondents.

The respondents were asked to give their assurance on whether they indulge in crime in future i.e. after release. The responses were presented in the following table.

TABLE 8.13

Assurance Regarding Future Crime

Assurance Given	*Frequency*	*Percentage*
Assurance Regarding Future Crime		
Would not indulge in crime	48	38.40
Indulge in crime	19	15.20
Do not know	28	22.40
No response	30	24.00
Total	**125**	**100.00**

It is observed that among the 125 respondents taken for the study, a considerable proportion of 48 respondents (38.40%) assured that they would not indulge in crime in future. But 19 respondents (15.20%) reiterated that they indulge in crime in future. It is also a sorry state that quite number of (28) respondents admitted that they could not give assurance of not indulging in crime since, they were very doubt about it.

TABLE 8.14

Assurance given and Nature of Crime Committed

Nature of Crime	*Assurance Given*			*Total*
	Not Indulge in crime	*Indulge in crime*	*Doubtful*	
Type I				
Murder	26	04	08	38
Non-murder	22	15	20	57
Total	**48**	**19**	**28**	**95***
Type II				
Involves victim	27	05	11	43
Non-victim	21	14	17	52
Total	**48**	**19**	**28**	**95***
Type III				
Against person	27	04	11	42
Against property	13	11	09	33
Against morality	08	04	08	20
Total	**48**	**19**	**28**	**95***
Type IV				
Convicts	43	12	20	75
Undertrials	05	07	08	20
Total	**48**	**19**	**28**	**95***
Type V				
Long termers	30	04	09	43
Short termers	18	15	19	52
Total	**48**	**19**	**28**	**95***

* Other 30 respondents did not respond and hence it is not applicable to them.

The responses were crossed with nature of crimes for further understanding and comparative purposes.

There were 95 responses for the above said enquiry out of 125 respondents. The remaining 30 respondents reiterated their stand of not accepting their crime and gave ultimately no response to this question.

There is no significant difference in distribution found between the respondents of murder related crimes and non-murder crimes on the respondents' assurance of not indulging in crime. Among the 19 respondents who admitted that they would indulge in crime majority of 15 were from crime relating to non-murder. Among those who could not decide (28), majority (20) of them belonged to non-murder related crime category. More or less similar trend has been observed among respondents belong to crime involves victim and no-victim categories.

Among the 48 respondents who assured that they would not indulge in crime in future, majority or 27 respondents were from crimes against person category. The 28 respondents who expressed doubt in giving assurance of not indulging in crime distributed more or less equally in all the three types of crimes viz., immorality, crime against person and crime against property though their proportion to the total sample of the study varies significantly.

Among the 52 short termers 19, 18 and 15 of them expressed doubt in giving assurance, not indulging in crime and reiterating their old behaviour of involving in criminal activities respectively.

Among the 75 convicts, 42 of them assured of not indulging in crime. There were 12 respondents who expressed of (20) respondents admitted that they could not judge whether they indulge in crime or not.

It is inferred from the above discussions that more assurance of not indulging in crime was observed among against person, convict and long termers than the respondents belong to non-murder, victimless crimes, immorality, property offences, short termers and under trial categories.

Difficulties Faced after Release

To understand how the respondents perceive the difficulties they face after release; the respondents were asked to report on that. The difficulties they would face include economical, familial, personal due to children and employment. These particulars may facilities for a successful rehabilitation programmes since the problems areas could be identified easily.

TABLE 8.15

Difficulties Faced after Release

Problems Faced After Release	*Frequency**
Economical	79
Personal	68
Familial	65
Children	62
Employment	16
Police	14
Others	04**
No problem	04

* Multiple response

** Includes medical-1, marriage-1 and problem due to husbands' second wife-2.

It is observed from the table that the respondents perceived that they would face problems in all spheres of life. Economical problem is one of the areas in which most of the respondents felt that they would face problems. It is quite clear and natural that their economical background and occupations were very low as observed while analysing their socio-economic conditions. The respondents who perceived that they would face personal problems after release is 68. The personal problems as reported by the respondents includes feeling of depression, disagrees and not known where to go after release. The respondents who felt that familial problems they would face along with other problems were 65. Which includes non-acceptance of family. Problems due to husband and relatives, absence of husband, problems relating to children and siblings; since respondents were branded as criminal. Those who perceive that children's education, upbringing, marriage would be one of the problems after release were 62. The employment (16) and police (14) would be problem for some of the respondents after release. Those who felt that police would be problem after release were mostly belong to crime relating to drug, illicit distillation and immoral offences. Hence most of them who felt that police would be a problem were, habitual offenders.

It is concluded that these problem areas could give some insight to the correction Jail officials to plan rehabilitation programmes in such a way to make it need based so as to be successful.

Help Expected from the Government

The respondents were very much eager to ask help from the government according to their needs. The following table explains the distribution of various types of help, assistance and guidance expected from the government by the respondents.

The Government mostly implies the prison and police departments to the respondents. The respondents expected various kinds of help includes effective vocational training (47), guidance (55), loan to start self employment activities (23) and release after they served a period of 10 years at the maximum (2). It is also noted that there were 21 respondents who had not expected any help from the Government.

TABLE 8.16

Help Expected from the Government

Help expected from Government	*Frequency**
Loan	52
Guidance	55
Vocational training	47
Employment	23
Want early release	02
No help expected	21

* Multiple response

9
Summary and Suggestions

Until recently the study of women criminals has been a neglected field of research though the phenomenon of the crime, women crime exit time immemorial. Low incidence of crime, fewer number of women criminals, low arrest rates and lack of interest are contributed much to this negligence. However, the incidence of crime is increasing. The tempo of urbanization and industrialization has altered the situation concerning female crime. The increasing trend among women criminality in the recent years and the interest on women and their development triggered the researchers to devote much attention on this complex phenomenon. The study on women criminals from varying perspectives made a conclusion that women criminals are conventional individuals or are mentally ill or are feeble minded or are like children.

The present study is intended to explore the women criminals from the social work perspectives. From the social work perspective, understanding of female criminals is vital for designing of policies and programmes related to them. Moreover social work in correction is a new development that stands in conformity with the present day philosophy of penal reformation which stress upon the treatment and rehabilitation of imprisoned women. Social workers in co-operation with the prison staff may help in setting right the prisoners in keeping them to lead a law abiding and socially purposeful life after release.

There has been a tendency to conceptualize crime in general terms which many a time lead to confusion in understanding. In the present study the respondents were classified into possible types on the basis of nature of crime and nature of sentence with a view to make an elaborate understanding.

Emphasis was given to the contributory role of the socio-cultural antecedents of the respondents. Moreover, details of family of orientation, family of procreation, details of husbands and marriage particulars are studied to have an indepth knowledge. The details of crime committed and the causes were also analysed indepth. The consequences of crime and its aftermath effect on individual, children, family and society at large as felt and/or experienced by the respondents were measured on a five point scale. The facilities available in the prison, the satisfaction level of the respondents on these facilities, impact of prison life, future plan after release and the respondents suggestions for improvement in the present prison conditions are dealt with in detail so to suggest a suitable prevention, treatment and rehabilitation programmes.

A. Personal Profile

The majority of respondents (70.40%) belonged to the age group of below 40 years with a range of 18 to 80 years. The mean age is 36.24 with a standard deviation of 12.05 and thus implying young and middle aged women's involvement in criminal activities. A considerable proportion (21.60%) of respondents belonged to the age group of above 45 years with the mean age of 54.93 shows that not only young and middle but also the old aged women's involvement in crimes.

Educational status of the respondents revealed that majority of 66.40 per cent were illiterates. However, a notable feature in the present study is that 33.60 per cent of the women were literates with either primary (8.80%) or middle (12.80%) or high school (8.00%) or higher secondary and above (4.00%) with a mean year of schooling as 2.03 years. Thus, a major proportion of two thirds of illiterates apparently reiterates the need for urgent and compulsory education for women.

According to the distribution of respondents by marital status, fifty per cent of the respondents belonged to the married category while one third are widows, one tenth were separated and the remaining 4.00 per cent were unmarried. The respondents by caste showed that nearly fifty per cent of them belonged to the backward caste (48.00%) and little above one fourth (28.40%) of them belonged to most backward caste. The scheduled caste comprises little less than one fourth (23.20%) of the sample. The distribution of the respondents by caste shows the high involvement of backward caste in crime.

When the religion of the respondents were taken into consideration the vast majority of 80.60 per cent belonged to Hindu religion. There were also respondents from Christian (12.00%) and Muslim (6.40%) religions.

The occupational status of the sample showed that 39.20 per cent were occupied as agricultural coolie/manual worker. One sixth (16.00%) were agriculturists while little more than one tenth (12.80%) were involved in trade, business or services. One out often (11.20%) were engaged in traditional occupations. However, nine respondents quoted illegal activations as their 'profession' while the remaining accounted for irregular employment and unemployment.

The income of the respondents revealed that nearly half of them (48.80%) earned a monthly income of Rs. 251-500. One sixth (16.80%) earned below Rs. 250 while one fifth (20.80%) earned between Rs. 501 and 750. The remaining earn more than Rs. 750. The computed mean income is Rs. 534.56

with the range of Rs. 60 to Rs. 3,000 with a standard deviation of Rs. 434.80, which inferred that majority of them were employed in lower paid occupations.

The residence of the respondents before and after marriage are taken into consideration, in order to know whether any linkages found between the domicile and crime. It was found that majority of 74.40 per cent of the respondents were from rural areas and the remaining one third of them belonged to urban areas. When the residence before marriage was taken into consideration more or less same trend has been observed even after marriage.

B. Personal Profile and Nature of Crime

For better understanding the personal profile was compared with the nature of crime committed by the respondents. For the purpose of the study the respondents were classified under five sets of types of crime. They are, (1) Crimes relating to murder and non-murder, (2) Crimes involving victim and no-victim, (3) Crime against property and other, and immorality, (4) Short-term prisoners and long-term prisoners and (5) Convicts and under trials.

For the purpose of comparative analysis the personal profile of the respondents were categorised as follows. Since the age is one of the crucial factor and distributed widely between 18 to 80, the age groups were kept as it is for comparing it with nature of crime. The educational status has been categorised into illiterates and literates. The marital status has been categorised, widow and separated. The religion has been categorised into Hindu and non-Hindu. The caste has been categorised into low caste and high caste. The low caste comprises of scheduled caste and most backward caste and the high caste includes backward caste and forward caste. Since the income level is widely distributed it was kept as it is.

(i) Age

Higher proportion of respondents who were above 45 years found a prominent place in crimes relating to murder, crimes involving victim, convicts and long termers. It is also found that when the age increases the proportion of respondents in long-term category increases in the short-term category increases. This implies the involvement of middle aged and old aged persons in the serious crimes are more.

(ii) Education

There is no difference between the distribution of respondents by their educational background and crimes relating to murder and non-murder, crimes involving victim and no-victim, crime against person, crime against property and immorality.

(iii) Marital Status

Majority of the married category respondents (60.31%) belonged to non-murder category while 'others' category respondents belonged fifty percentages each in murder category. There is no difference of distribution between respondents marital status and crimes involving victim and no-victim.

There is more or less equal percentage of distribution found between both married and 'others' categories of respondents as far as the crime against person, crime against property and immorality is concerned.

(iv) Caste and Religion

It is concluded that the proportion of low caste respondents (58.06%) was high in crimes relating to non-murder than murder (41.94%). Both low caste and high caste respondents were distributed more or less equally in crimes involving victim and no-victim. There is not much difference found between low caste and high caste respondents as far as the crime against person, crime against property and immorality. It is also inferred that involvement of 'high caste' people in criminal activities is on the increase. Both low caste and high caste represented equally among long termers and short termers. The respondents were distributed equally in both crimes involving victim and no-victim respective of their religion. Moreover there is no significant difference in distribution of respondents by religion as far as the crime against person, crime against property and immorality and, convicts and under trials and concerned.

(v) Monthly Income

It is concluded that the respondents belonging to the higher income level commit murder related crime and *vice versa*. There is no significant difference found between the distribution of the respondents as far as crimes involving victim and no-victim. In other words, the respondents were more or less equally distributed in crimes involving victim and no-victim irrespective of their income level. Major proportion of the respondents (48.40%) were distributed in the income category of Rs. 251-500 irrespective of whether involved in crime against person, crime against property and immorality. More or less same ratio of convicts and under trials (as in the study sample is 3 : 1) is observed in all the income categories except in upto Rs. 250 category. It is also observed that both short termers and long termers were more or less equally distributed in all the income categories except in Rs. 501-750 and above Rs. 750 categories. In the Rs. 501-750 category, major proportion belonged to short termers and the trend is reversed in the next income category of Rs. 750 and above, thus conforming, that the high level of income of the respondents is associated with serious offences.

(vi) Respondents—Before and After Marriage

The rural respondents tend to commit crimes relating to

murder than crimes relating to non-murder while the urban respondents tend to commit crimes relating to non-murder than the crimes relating to murder both either before or after marriage are concerned. In the urban area higher proportion of the respondents were observed in crimes involving no-victim than victim involving crimes. It is also found that the respondents with urban background were distributed triple times higher in crimes involving no-victim than in crimes involving victim category. The respondents were more or less equally distributed in both crimes involving victim and no-victim irrespective of their rural-urban background when the residence before or after marriage is concerned.

In crimes against person, crimes against property and immorality the rural respondents were higher than the urban respondents. The rural respondents dominated in crimes against person while urban respondents dominated in crimes against property and immorality both before and after marriage.

It is concluded that the same ratio (as in the study sample 3 : 1) for convicts and under trials prevails with regard to the domicile of respondents either before or after marriage. There is no significant difference in distribution found between the rural respondents and their term of imprisonment while a notable difference was found between the urban respondents and their term of imprisonment. The urban respondents constitute a high proportion in short-term imprisonment, thus, implies that their involvement in crimes relating to property, immorality, drug etc., for which the punishment period is also relatively shorter. Both long termers and short termers were distributed more or less equally between rural and urban when their residence after marriage is taken into consideration.

C. Family of Orientation

Majority of the respondents belong to the family size of 5 and more children, indicating overcrowding in their families.

In this study it is also observed that majority of sixty per cent of respondents had lived in family of pattered and overcrowding type. The respondents from single parent home constitute one third of the total. The above findings suggest that these respondents were brought up in a family situation where uncongenial situation prevailed which hindered their fullest development to some extent.

With regard to the type of the family most of the respondents belonged to nuclear type. It is also observed that nearly fifty per cent of the respondents were brought up by single parents and relatives; which might have a considerable influence on the socialization of the individual.

In more than fifty per cent of respondents' family either one or more members were educated. A considerable proportion of respondents' families' mean educational score is one in the sense that these families have no illiterates.

(i) Parental Treatment and Residential Description

It was observed that in 50 per cent of the respondents' family both male and female children were treated equally. When the preferential treatment, if any, shown by the parents were reported, more than fifty per cent of the respondents' family showed to the male than the females in the area of love, care, security, education, employment, marriage and property.

More than 50 per cent of the respondents are from populated families. A vast majority of respondents were brought up in a narrow, congested and less spacious house environment. Moreover, majority of 76.8 per cent of respondents were brought up in a poor economic condition. It is important to note that there were 11.2 per cent of respondents who exposed to criminal risk during their childhood days. It is reported that 34.4 per cent of the quarrelsome in nature. This might have contributed in one way or the other in ineffective socialization of the respondents.

(ii) Sibling Position

Almost an overwhelming majority of 64.40 per cent of the respondents were born with one or more siblings. Three out of ten (28.80%) were first born while one fifth (21.60%) were second born to their parents. About one third (32.00%) were middle born and one out of ten (11.20%) were the last born in their family. From the above findings it is inferred that there is no relationship between siblings position and criminal behaviour.

Majority of the respondents were employed in low paid occupation and irregular employment. As reported by the respondents, among those who were employed 22.83 per cent had to shift their occupation due to salary, illtreatment and unsatisfactory work environment. But there were only two respondents, who reported that their employees' illtreatment was also one of the contributory causes for their criminal behaviour.

(iii) Details of Guardian

It is found that the guardians of major of respondents (77.78%) were illiterates and were engages in manual, irregular occupation or unemployed. This might had considerable bearing on the respondents.

(iv) Childhood Criminal Behaviour

It is observed that one fifth of the respondents' childhood friends and one third of the relatives had criminal record. A meager percentage (2.40%) of the respondents involved in criminal activity along with their parent/guardian, among whom two were trained for the purpose.

D. Family of Procreation

Majority of the respondents belonged to the family size of 2 to 4 members. There were sixty six per cent of the respondents whose family members were educated.

When the educational level of the family members is crossed with nature of crime it was observed that the involvement of persons in crime from educated family is on the increase. It is also observed that there was no relationship between the type of crime committed and the educational level of the family.

(i) Age at Marriage

When the marital age difference between the respondents and husbands was calculated it showed a difference from 10 to 13 years. More over, majority of the respondents (70.83%) who married before they attained 18 years, imply that these women were not physically and mentally matured enough to cop with the expectations of the family of procreation.

(ii) Status of Marriage

Vast majority of 70.83 per cent of the respondents were enjoying the status of first wife while the remaining 29.17 per cent were either second wife or concubine. The difference is high between the respondents and husbands who married for second and third time. It was inferred that marrying more than once or frequent marriages are attributed with maladjustments, misunderstanding and conflicts among the partners.

(iii) Illegal Relations and Conflict

More than one fourth (26.40%) of the respondents and little less than fifty per cent (46.67%) of the husbands had illegal relationship witn other persons. It is interesting to note that there were 18 spouses who had illegal relationship outside their wedlock.

There were 55 per cent of respondents who had conflict with their husbands. The respondents also faced illtreatment from husbands (50.83%), parents-in-law (23.33%), other in-laws (15.83%) and other relatives of husbands (14.17%). The various forms of illtreatment includes attempt to murder, beating, scolding, house arrest, not allowing to meet the husband, starving, quarrelling etc.

(iv) Details of Husbands

Among those employed skilled and technical service were the occupations for 50 per cent of the respondents' husbands. More than one third of the respondents' husbands (36.49%) were engaged in low paid occupations like agricultural coolie and other physical manual work.

The mean monthly income of the respondents' husbands is Rs. 746.80 with a standard deviation of Rs. 1274.78 and it ranged from Rs. 200 to Rs. 10,000. The habits and behaviour of the husbands showed that six out of ten (61.67%) were alcoholics and three out of ten (29.17%) were drug addicts. A little less than half (35.83%) were indulging in criminal activities. Among those who indulge in criminal activities only 31.67 per cent had criminal record. It was also observed that 14.17 per cent of the husbands were imprisoned for their criminal activities at the time of the study.

E. Crime Committed

Nearly fifty per cent of the respondents had committed crimes relating to murder and, more or less equal proportion of the respondents were involved in crimes relating to non-murder.

It was found that equal halves of the total respondents either accepted or did not accept their crime. One third (35.20%) of the respondents felt that they were falsely implicated in the case either by neighbours (29.55%) or by police (22.73%) or by others.

The district-wise distribution showed that the respondents were widely distributed in almost all the districts of Tamil Nadu. A considerable proportion of respondents were from Madurai (22.40%) district.

Half of the respondents committed the crime on or before two years and the rest prior to three or more years. More than half (56.00%) of the respondents had committed crime when they were below the age of 30 years and the rest of them were middle and old aged offenders.

Among those who committed crimes relating to murder, 67.39 per cent of the respondents played main role in executing the criminal act. This implied that they were more aggressive and have toughness as par with male in committing crime. Exactly 50 per cent of the respondents had done the crime all alone and the remaining half had committed crime with the help of associates. Majority of the respondents' accomplice (86.95%) were relatives or family members as far as crimes relating to murder is concerned.

Four out of ten (40.00%) were imprisoned for murder. A little less than one fifth (19.20%) of them were involved in illicit distillation and one sixth (16.00%) of them were imprisoned for immorality. Respondents also indulged in drug related crimes (11.20%), theft (4.00%) and quarrelling (2.40%).

Among the causes reported by the respondents, economical causes found a predominant place. It includes unemployment (51), low income (48), poverty (47) and property dispute (9). The personal causes were listed by the respondents as to luxurious life (48), to make more money (42), emotional reason (17), self-defence (9), for survival (4) and conflict with daughter. Both illegitimacy and illtreatment have also played a crucial role in motivating the respondents to involve in criminal activities. It is also noted that many a time the respondents reported either single cause or more than one causes. The mean cause is worked out as 3.21.

F. Details of Murderers

Among the 56 respondents who involved in crimes relating to murder, 50 were murderers. Among them committed triple murder, one committed double murder and other two were involved in dowry murder. The rest of six respondents involved in attempted murder (3), accomplice in murder (2) and one attempted for self-immolation.

It is found that the victims were close relatives and persons known to them. However a notable proportion (18.18%) of victims were outsiders and persons unknown to the respondents. Majority of the murder and murder related crimes were done alone (58.93%). There were 73.21 per cent of the respondents who played the main role in executing the crime. This explain their increasing prominent role and aggressiveness and toughness as equalled with men in committing crimes. Most of the accomplice involved were close relatives and persons well known to them. Considerable proportion of the respondents (47.27%) used sharp edged weapons for committing murder crimes and murder related crimes.

G. Details of Non-Murders

The respondents who committed crimes relating to non-murder category comprise 55.20 per cent in the study sample. The crimes were illicit distillation (34.78%), immorality (28.99%), theft related crimes (07.25%), and other crimes (08.70%).

Respondents who committed crime related to illicit distillation were observed as highest frequent offenders than other crimes. Among these respondents a major proportion had committed crimes more than 26 items.

A vast majority of 73.91 per cent of respondents played the main role in executing the crime relating to non-murder. Among those, the number of cases which involves an accomplice accounted for 57.94 per cent. It is further observed that most of the accomplices were husband (32.50%), relatives (25.00%) and friends and colleagues (27.5%).

One out of ten (10.4%) surrendered to the police. They surrendered due to reasons like conscience, fear of punishment, neighbours and relatives initiation and hoping for a reduction in punishment.

H. Consequences on Individual, Children, Family and Society

The consequences are broadly classified into four areas, viz., consequences on individual, children, family and society at large. In each area ten important factors were identified and listed in the schedule. These ten factors were measured using a Likert type five point scale. It is important to note that these identified factors do not necessarily have any impact directly on the respondents due to their criminal behaviour and after-math effects. It is the question of how they felt and/or experienced in their life.

(i) On Individual

Majority of the respondents with a mean score ranged from 3.92 to 4.86 agreed that academic life, social status, personal life, and individual freedom are affected due to their criminal behaviour and aftermath effects. Majority of the respondents fully agreed that crime involves financial loss. Most of the respondents agreed fully that criminals feel depressed and detached from the family and society. It is concluded that the respondent perceived consequences on the individual is high. The mean score ranged from 3.92 to 4.56 which implied that majority of the respondents felt and/or experienced the consequences of crime at the individual level.

(ii) On Children

Most of the respondents have fully agreed that their

criminal conduct and its effect on their children is adverse. They agreed that children's upbringing, Education, morality and personality development is affected by parents criminal conduct. A vast majority of the respondents agreed that the children of the offender faced social harassment and exposure to criminal risk. By indulging in criminal activities, the offender lose control over the children and prove to be negative model to them. Major proportion of respondents fully agreed with the importance of the role of the mother in upbringing the children in family. The mean score rated by the respondents ranged from 3.82 to 4.68.

(iii) On Family

Most of the respondents have fully agreed that their siblings future life, status of the family and neighbours relationships have been affected by the criminal behaviour. They also fully agreed that their criminal behaviour results in the mental agony of parents or parents-in-law. They agreed ultimately lead to disintegration of the family when one of its member is indulged in criminal activities. The marital life of both criminal and his or her partner have been adversely affected by the criminal activity. This contention has been supported by majority of the respondents. The family factors. Which suffer a negative effect due to criminal behaviour of the members, have been rated with a mean score ranging from 3.82 to 4.62.

(iv) On the Society

It is found that respondents were of the opinion that the criminal behaviour of the member have considerable influence on the society. It is reported that due to criminal behaviour the social participation have been lessened. The respondents were aware that criminal act have done much harm to the community and the Government. More over they also agreed that the criminal behaviour results in loss to the government.

It is also seen that the respondents agreed that the criminals sow seed to a problematic society and ultimately the society gets polluted. It is interesting to note that most of the respondents did not agree to the contention that the criminal behaviour results in law and order problem.

From the overall findings of the consequences it is strange to note that though majority of the respondents agreed that the consequences on the individual level, on aware of the consequences on the social structure, some of them would like to indulge in crime in future, suggests that urgent remedial steps have to be taken to prevent these women from involving in crime any more.

I. Prison Life

It was observed that the facilities provided in prison such as food, accommodation, bathing, clothing, medical recreation, educational vocational training, work incentives, grievance redressal and other facilities were not satisfactory. The mean score of satisfaction level ranges from 1.22 to 2.34. It is understood from the mean scores that these facilities are grossly ineffective and can play only an ineffective role in rehabilitating the prisoners.

The distribution of the respondents by punishment period showed that about two fifths (38.40%) are imprisoned for more than 14 years, of which six were sentenced to life imprisonment. Above one tenth (12.80%) were sentenced for more than three months and less than a year. A notable proportion of one third (36.00%) were punished for less than three months.

More than half (53.60%) of the respondents reported that they were visited by either relatives or friends or both. However, one third (35.20%) reported that they had no visitors for them. Among those who have visitors, four out of ten (43.20%) had visitors either once in a month (22.39%) or fortnightly (20.90%). One third (32.84%) were visited either half yearly (17.91%) or once in a year (14.93%).

The impact of prison life on respondents showed that four out of ten (40.80%) felt that prison life helped them in one way or the other. Of those, majority of three fourths (74.51%) admitted that prison life changed their bad character and criminal attitude. One fifth (20.00%) felt no help from prison life. Contradict to this one third (36.84%) opined prison life as punishment oriented than rehabilitating and 21.40 per cent reported that prison life harmful.

Poor quality and quantity of food, dress and cosmetics top among the problems faced by the prisoners, lack of privacy was reported by 96 respondents while improper care was quoted by 102 respondents. Want of recreation and communication facilities was reiterated by 95 respondents.

An array of suggestion were given by the respondents. Improvement in quality and quantity on items such as food, dress, cosmetics, etc., were stressed by 112 respondents. Vocational training, educational programmes, guidance centres and marginal incentives were felt necessary and important by 98 respondents while 108 have requested for improvement in medical facility was suggested by 76 respondents while treatment, redressal and care was reiterated in form of suggestion by 120 respondents.

J. Future Plan

It is found that one third of the respondents each proposed to stay with their parents and husbands after release. Though 50 per cent of the respondents in our study sample had lived with their husbands before coming to the prison, a considerable proportion have proposed to live with their parents. This indicates the prevalence of conflicts and maladjustments in their married life.

Majority of the respondents would like to be employed in menial and casual labour. Nearly one fourth of the respondents wanted to start self-employment activities such as petty shop, vegetable shop, fruit stall and other small business activities. A major proportion who would like to engage in low paid occupation implied the ineffectiveness of the vocational training available to them in prison. There were one tenth of the respondents who wanted to continue their criminal professions. This implied that the prison life has no impact on changing and rehabilitating the prisoners.

K. Acceptance of Family and Society

There were 56 per cent of respondents who felt that their family would accept them after release. In the same way there were only 21.60 per cent who felt that the society would accept them after release. A considerable proportion (40.00%) and three fourths (75.20%) felt that the family and society would not accept them after release. When the perceived acceptance of the family and society by the respondents is compared with the nature of crime, it is observed that most of the respondents who committed crime relating to murder, involving victim and crime against person felt that they would be accepted by their family than the society. It is also understood from the responses that the crime relating murder, involving victim and against person are done most of the time for the benefit of the family.

The respondents under crimes relating to non-murder, involving no-victim, crime against property, immorality, drug related crimes etc., have perceived themselves as miscreants in the family and society and so the respondents involved in these types of crimes, in many cases, perceived that they would not be accepted by the family and society.

As far as the acceptance of the society is concerned the respondents were of the opinion that whether the crime relating to murder or non-murder, crimes involving victim or no-victim and crime against person and property and immorality, it makes no difference to the society.

L. Assurance Given

There were 38.40 per cent of the respondents who assured that they would not indulge in crime in future while 15.20 per cent reported that they would indulge. It is strange to note that there were 22.40 per cent who could not give any assurance whether they would indulge in crime or not.

When the assurance given by the respondents is compared with the nature of the crime committed, it was observed that those who committed crimes relating to murder, crimes involving victim, crime against person were higher than the other type of offenders. The majority of respondents who committed crimes involving no-victim, relating to non-murder, against property and immorality have reported that they would either indulge in crime or doubtful in giving assurance.

M. Suggestion for Improvement

The following suggestions are drawn in order to prevent people from indulging in crime and to give better treatment and rehabilitation for those who already entered into the criminal system. The suggestions are classified under two headings as suggestions for prevention and suggestions for effective welfare and rehabilitative programmes.

(i) Prevention

In planning up the programme for the prevention of crime it should first be borne in mind that human nature is complex and programmes must be in accordance with. Many are of the opinion that crime prevention is the task of the police and justice system alone. Insofar as crime is a social phenomenon crime prevention is the responsibility of every part of the society (The President's Commission Report, 1967 p. 1). Prevention of crime is not only the responsibility of the police and the criminal justice system but also the general public. Hence the co-operation of the public in crime prevention programme must be incorporated.

The sociological approach which calls for the establishment of pre-delinquent contacts with a view to spot out criminal tendencies and prevent their growth on one hand and elimination of the factors favourable to crime on the other must be given due emphasis.

The various methods such as educating the public through mass media, community programmes, participation of youth and children in communication and education programmes like small group discussions and critical incidence programmes must be employed. The role of the voluntary organisations could be of immense use in prevent of crime.

The school children could be the largest target groups there the criminal tendencies can be spot out on the national level. The children can be educated from the school level onwards. For those who do not go to school non-formal educational institutions and voluntary organisations could be used for the purpose.

(ii) Police Social Work Team Model

Those who need the services of the criminal justice system frequently require something other than the legal or law enforcement remedies (Treger, *et. al.* 1974). As developed in United States by Treger and others (1974) a Police Social work Team Model could be established at the district level to provide social assessment, 24 hours crisis intervention, services to police could be started. The team can also receive consultative services from legal and psychiatric whenever needed.

The main purpose of the project established in United States was to demonstrate that speedy social assessment and early intervention to initiate treatment immediately by diverting some non-violent misdemeanants and others to a more appropriate social resource of the community or to a social worker in the police department. The project found that police-social work co-operation enhanced the function of both professions. Social workers in a police department provided immediate and early services at critical times. Hence, such a team model in Indian settings no doubt prove to be successful in providing social assessment, crisis intervention, treatment, referral services, short-term and long-term individual counselling, marital counselling, family and group therapy and group services to the clients who may be referred by the police and also who approach voluntarily.

N. Welfare and Rehabilitation Programmes

The welfare services must be started when a women criminal enter into the prison system and complete when she age in gets settled into the society. She should be treated as an individual and as part of the society with a view to improve her personality and behaviour. It is an urgent need to recognise women prisoners as a distinct social group. For successful welfare and rehabilitative programmes, the following suggestions are given.

The quality and quantity of food provided are very poor as reported by the respondents. Most of them were not satisfied with the food and accommodation. It is one of the important suggestions footforth by majority of the respondents. The food commodities provided to the prisoners can be improved in its quality and quantity periodically by improving the menu. The problem of accommodation in the form of overcrowding can be tackled by providing adequate number of cells.

(i) Medical and Psychiatric Treatment

The correctional medical and mental health services can play a constructive part in the rehabilitation of the prisoners right from the moment the prisoner is admitted in a penitentiary. The person may come inside with feelings of guilt and fear, resentment, self pity, relief and remorse and helplessness. It is here that medical and psychiatric services are very much in need. To provide such facilities hospitals with well equipped facilities are of crucial need. The medical officer should be available for that purpose with all necessary para-medical staff who may be available for that purpose with during day and night. Health services should be provided in taking into consideration the inmates' biological, medical psychological and emotional problems. Expectant mothers and children should be given adequate care. For the expectant mothers pre-natal and post-natal care, nutritious food and medical check up are necessary. For the children creche and nursery schools must form part of the welfare services.

Together with the medical treatment psychiatric services such as individual therapy, group therapy, therapy of maturity, therapy of research and therapy of conditional fear be adequately available to the women criminals. When these services are provided, in long run these facilities facilitate rehabilitation process much easier. As Ansari (1982) pointed out, a person on admission in a prison is an emotionally disturbed being, he/she is a bundle of nerves and worries. He/she becomes neurotic and labours under the notions of persecution and hallucinations. As a result, she develops split personalities. The behaviour of the custodial staff adds to the frustration of the inmates and many a time they react in a natural but unfavourable manner to the fears, anxieties and frustrations of the hostile prisoners under the name of controlling and guiding them. Almost all the prisoners need counselling and hence psychiatric social workers shall be posted in all women prisons. Apart from counselling, referral services like educational programmes. Vocational training, work therapy and recreational programmes are also made available.

(ii) Educational Programmes

The need for education is every where appreciable various studies conducted in prisons revealed that most the prisoners are illiterates. The present study also supports the findings of the earlier studies. Hence providing educational programmes including adult education is very much essential. The educational services fulfill the twin objectives-on the part of the prisoner improving the educational standard and on the part of the prison officials correctional work is much easier if the prisoners are illiterates. By educational programmes the semi-illiterates can have an opportunity to continue their studies. To wit, those who finished schooling can go for higher studies, Educational programmes shall consist of library, workshop gymnasium moral education classes and religious education.

(iii) Vocational Training

Most of the prison departments have their own industry set up in the prison to make use of the prison labour. In most of the places the traditional trades such as cloth weaving, tape weaving, durrie weaving, niwar weaving, wool carding, carpet weaving, carpentry, blacksmithy, knitting and polyester industry are also set up. For the prisoners fixed wages are given for their labour as an incentive. These industries were started with a short-term objective that they learn and earn money and make use of their labour potential and with a long run objective of making the prisoners self sufficient in such a way that these trades should be useful to earn their bread after release.

A separate training for them in prison must be developed

keeping in mind the social and economic role of women in the society.

Training should be imparted only after identifying the training needs of women prisoners. The traditional methods of training like bidi making, niwar making, durrie making etc., should be replaced by modern and latest occupations which would fetch an employment after release.

Before giving guidance and training, assessment of their socio-economic background, educational qualification and capacities should be done systematically. To bring out a healthy psychological development among the individual prisoners training in their choice and payment of adequate remuneration for the work done is important. Training programmes need to be organised with the help of experts and implemented by trained supervisory persons. From the present study it is found that there is no vocational training in Madurai Women Prison. Added to this there is no provision for utilizing the prison labour. Idleness is reported as one of the greatest problems of Madurai prisoners. Hence provisions shall be made both for vocational training and prison labour.

(iv) Recreational Services

Recreational services are more necessary for the prisoners as their life is confined to four walls with a routine work. Added to this living away from the family and community give them the feeling of depression. In order to have a free mind, recreational facilities should be provided. Along with radio and television, musical programmes, cultural programmes and film shows should also be arranged periodically. Various sports and games materials shall also be made available to exhibit their talents.

(v) Social Case Work

Social case work is one of the important methods in social work. It has a distinguished role to play in the prisoner.

By case work methods the individual finds the problem area and also tries to find out solution for that problem along with the cooperation of the case worker. The slowly winning the confidence of the individual in such a way that the person may identify his own problem area. The case work programme should be started immediately when a person enters the prison.

(vi) Re-integration Programmes

The ultimate aim of setting up of prison and providing them the welfare and rehabilitate services are to make the prisoners behave in a socially acceptable manner and settle again in the society as a normal being. Hence the prisoner should not be isolated from the community once for all. Often arrangement are to be made to facilitate the contacts of family members, relatives and friends, allowing them to attend family and social functions etc. Open air prison instead of making them living within four walls is a bold step in this regard. Weekend programmes can be organised periodically so as to make the family members and husbands meet the imprisoned women occasionally. Such programmes may form part of the pre-release preparation for their re-socialization and re-integration into the society. These programmes make the prisoner to have a feeling of being with the community. The prison life in any way should not cut off her links with the community.

After the release, the prisoners are to be settled in the society socially, economically and emotionally. Follow up programmes play a crucial role in this regard. It is rather very difficult to change the attitude of the community towards the prisoners. Educating both the community and the released persons make the after care services more effective. The help of the voluntary agencies and private institutions may very well be sought in this regard.

After release, these women should be looked after adequately and considerable help should be extended so that they will not indulge in crime in future. In after care programmes not only their economic needs but also social and psychological needs must be given due consideration. Government sponsored counselling centres to help the women in coping with their inter-personal problems may be set up at different places.

Follow up study of such released prisoners should be made to asses the impact of rehabilitative programmes so as to identify the problem areas and to make improvements in the programmes. The ultimate aim of rehabilitative programmes are to make the women criminals to be accepted by the husband, family and society where they originally belong. This could be possible by changing the attitude of the husband, family and society by way of educating them and creating an awareness.

10
Indian Prisons—Need for New Dimension

Prison for the adult criminals and approved or certified schools for the young offenders have been created to keep them for the convicted period. The present law enforcement system and the justice system order the criminals to be kept in the prison for a specific period depending on the crime. The prison is a place of punishment. The prison instead of being a place of punishment it should become a correctional setting. It should bring the criminal into a more harmonious and or sympathetic attitude towards society.

The objective of a prison as stated in Gladstone Committee of 1985 is that it should have as its primary and concurrent objects, deterrence and reformation and that the task of the prison service should be to release offenders as better men and women both physically and morally, than when they came in.

The mission statement for English Prison Board is that the prison services serves the public by keeping in custody those committed by the courts. Out duty is to look after them with humanity and to help them lead law-abiding and useful lives in custody and after release.

The Indian Jail Committee report suggested that the aim

of the prison administration should further be to effect such a reformation in the character of criminal and will fit him again to take his place in society and become a useful citizen.

Florence Nightingale once said that the first requisite of a hospital was that it made the patients no worse. It seems, therefore, that a minimum criterion of prison effectiveness should be that an inmate should emerge no worse than when he or she enters.

The impact of prison life on the individual is not so much to reform the prisoner but to prevent him from being ruined by the treatment given by the prison authorities because prison is considered as a punitive model than a treatment model. The prisoner happens to commit a crime and sent to the jail where in the situation should help him to repent and become a new person.

There are studies on the status of the prison and the prisoners, which point out that the prison has to enable the inmates to change his attitude, habits and to become a person who will be accepted by the society. Therefore the rehabilitation of the offenders should be an important role of the prison and the prison officials. The prison officials could reform and rehabilitate prisoners if they were given more funding to upgrade facilities, personnel and programmes and prisons.

Dunbar (1985) enunciated three principles known as individualism, relationship and activity in the prison life. Good prison regimes flow from prisoners being treated as individuals from relationship between staff and prisoners being good and from prisoners being active rather than idle in the cells.

Individualism of an individual irrespective of his crime and the inter personal relationship between the authorities and as well as with the inmates with the active involvement of the prisoners to keep them busy instead idle are essential to reform a criminal. In other words it should lead humane containment.

The offenders have a right to humane rather than inhumane imprisonment and the prison services should ensure that genuinely humane conditions are achieved for all prisoners throughout the system. But at the same time humane containment should not lead to human warehouses.

The individual prisoners are being treated differently and trained which should be replaced by a positive custody. It is to create an environment, which can assist the prisoners to respond and contribute to society as positively as possible.

Justice and welfare as concepts are not opposites or mirror images of one another, with justice not committed to welfare and welfare becoming unjust. In fact the requirement of looking after the welfare of inmates certainly includes an obligation to treat them with justice and *vice versa*. Yet the two terms are not strictly synonymous.

The growth of criminals or the increasing prison population or the crime escalating not only in sheer size but also in complexity with no sign of recidivism declining significantly.

The offenders who are kept in prison form a community within a community. This is a temporary community for reconciliation and rehabilitation. In the prison the inmates are given opportunity to engage themselves in certain jobs, which are to learn the skills. When the prisoners are released after completing their period of conviction this skill may help them to become independent for their living. But it is quite often noticed whenever there is a common prison for both the sexes the women prisoners are given the job of housekeeping and preparation of food for the inmates. This has only kept the women in their traditional and routine work as they were in their homes before committing the crime. Therefore the rehabilitation measure is seldom provident to the female offenders.

Since in most of the prisons are meant for both the sexes such limitations are unavoidable from a general perception. But the women criminals are to be prepared to be fit to live in the society after their conviction, which is very gloomy.

Moreover not only male members but also the female members commit the crimes. There is no discrimination that only male members or female members are committing only certain crimes. Any type of crime both sexes are being represented of course the male criminals may be more in number than the female criminals.

Women Offenders—Recent Developments

It may not be wrong to stage that a woman committed the first crime in the world by violating the God's command as per the Christian doctrine. The criminality among the women is on the increase. The women offenders are found in almost all the fields on par with the male offenders.

The past four decades have seen our society virtually saturated with crime, sensationalism, sadism, sex and brutality. Broken homes, conflicts and unhappy intra familial relations, widening of spheres of occupational and social activities, radio, movies, TV, widespread circulation of pornographic literature each has inadvertently contributed to criminality among women.

Women offenders come to the notice of the police mostly for shoplifting, domestic theft, violation of Excise and Prohibition laws, prostitution and infanticide. In recent years, there is a rising trend of women taking part in offences of dacoit and white collar crime like cheating, criminal breach of trust, smuggling etc.

The young offenders or the juveniles who have been arrested under the Indian Penal Code (IPC) and Local and Special Laws (LSL) by sex reveal the alarming increase among the girls.

TABLE 10.1

Young Girl offenders Arrested under Cognizable IPC and LSL

Age Group	*Section*	*Year*				
		1985	*1986*	*1987*	*1988*	*1989*
7-12 Yrs.	IPC	110	146	141	127	162
	LSL	414	088	384	300	042
12- 16 Yrs.	IPC	379	407	528	630	549
	LSL	326	332	179	422	310
16-18 Yrs.	IPC	707	713	852	1794	2280
	LSL	811	9282	1673	1830	8272

The quantitative information shown in the above table is evident that the young girls are being trapped into the crime world and once they are branded and experienced the jail life they continue to be in the same field.

The National Crime Records Bureau came out the statistical information with regard to the women arrested in cognizable crime under local special law during the year 1988 was 1,49,332 as against 37,21,171 males arrested, the percentage of total being 96.1 males and 3.9 females. In the following year 1989, the total number of women arrested under LSL shot up to 1,74,574 as against 38,69,905 males arrested, the percentage of total being 95.7 males and 4.3 females. Highest number of women arrested was from Tamil Nadu, Maharashtra and Gujarat.

The reasons for the female offenders to commit a crime revolve around the family environment and the dissatisfaction encountered by the female members from the family members.

If they are married in most of the cases it is their better half who is the main cause for the women to become an offender. Though there is a belief that women have high tolerance level but even that is being burnt out and lead to commit a crime. The psychological dissatisfaction in the family situation which lead to stress has been observed as one of the main contributing factor for the female offenders.

Another important phenomenon about the female offenders is that they are not organized as a kind of gang as in the case of the male offenders. At tunes the women criminals in majority of the cases happen to be a single individual in committing a crime.

Highest number of women was arrested from Tamil Nadu for the crimes under Narcotic Drugs and Psychotropic Substances Act, Gambling, Prohibition Act, Immoral Traffic (Prevention) Act and Dowry Prohibition Act.

When compared with male criminality, the extent of female criminality denotes a perceptible movement. The total number of males arrested increased from 21,23,930 in 1985 to 22,35,381 in 1989, a rise of 5.24 per cent. In the same period female arrested increased from 56,480 in 1985 to 67,851 in 1989, a rise of 20.13 per cent.

The quantitative information with regard to the female offenders is a disturbing phenomenon at the same tune it should not be ignored. Since the population is increasing and the female members are almost equal in size as male members does not justify the increase in criminality among the females. When there is an increase in female offenders there are also other difficulties in handling the situation by the prison authorities as there are certain limitations.

Difficulties in Dealing with Women Offenders

Many offenders have dependent children or relatives who must be cared for and hence it has to be considered before during and after conviction of a female offender. At times when this is not taken into consideration the law enforcement authorities are being condemned for being inhumane in their dealing with the female offenders.

Institutional settings are to be created to keep the women offenders who are dangerous to themselves and others, or who are not capable of living in free and uncontrolled settings.

There is already a kind of discrimination in built in the society against the criminals and it is aggravated if they are female offenders. Acceptance of the ex-offenders in the family and in the community due to the stigma irrespective of gender is a major problems encountered by offenders in general and female offenders in particular. It further hampers the rehabilitation of the ex-offenders.

The societal treatment encountered by the women offenders after their conviction period is at times unbearable to the extent that they even resort to some means to end their life.

Therefore while the female offenders are in the prisons they have to be given capacity building on one side by providing skill oriented training and on the other increase their will power to face the society.

There are professionals like social workers who are trained to deal with problematic individuals to prepare them socially, psychologically to become a fit person in the society. Let us make use of their expertise and help the unfortunate and situations offenders to be a normal person to live in our society.

Bibliography

Abbot and Clare Wallace (1990). *An Introduction to Sociology: Feminist Perspectives*, Routledge, London.

Adler, Freda (1975). *Sisters in Crime*, McGraw Hill: New York, Houghten Mifflin Company, Boston.

Adwani, Nirmala H. (1978). *Perspectives on Adult Crime and Correction: A Comparative Study of Adult Prisoners and Probationers*, Abhinav Publications, New Delhi.

Ansari, M.A. (1981). *Mahila Paradhikya Evam Punarasthapan*, Panchsheel Prakashan, Jaipur.

Ansari, M.A. (1981). The Scope of Welfare Services in the Indian Prisons, *Social Defence*, Vol. XVII, No. 68.

Ahuja, Ram (1969). *Female Offenders in India*, Meenakshi Prakashan, Meerut.

Ahuja, Ram (1970). "Female Murderer in India: A Sociological Study", *Indian Journal of Social Work*, 31 (3), 272-84.

Aiyisha, A.R. (1988). *Women in Criminal Justice*, Paper presented at the Annual Conference of the Indian Society of Criminology, March 4-6.

All India Committee on Jail Reforms, 1980-83.

Arora, J.C. and Surat Mishra (1983). *Crime Against Women*, Bureau of Police Research and Development, New Delhi.

Ashok Kumar, N. and Lakshmipathy, V. Jully (1986). *Social Defence*, National Institute of Social Defence, Ministry of Welfare, Government of India, Vol. XXII.

Barnes, H.E. and Teetere, N.K. (1944). *New Horizons in Criminology*, New York.

Baybach, P.J. (1977). "Women Offenders: A Commentary on Current Conceptions of Women in Crime", *Quarterly Journal of Corrections*, Vol. 1, No. 4, Fall.

Bhanot, M.L. and Surat Mishra, (1978). *Criminality Amongst Women*, Bureau of Police Research and Development, Government of India, New Delhi.

Bhanot, M.L. and Surat Mishra, (1980). *Criminality Amongst Women in India (A study of Female Offenders and Female Convicts)*, Bureau of Police Research and Development, New Delhi.

Bhattacharyya, (1992). "Crime: Its Causes and Remedies", *Employement News, August*, Vol. XVII, No. 19, New Delhi.

Biddle, B.J. (1986). Recent Developments in Role Theory, *American Sociological Review*, 12, pp. 67-92.

Blumberg, S.A. (1971). *Crime Justice in America, in Crime and Justice in America*, (ed.) Jack, D. Douglas Indianpolis, The Bobbs-Merrill Company.

—*Amongst Women*, Bureau of Police Research and Development, Government of India, New Delhi.

Boehm, W.W. (1959). *The Social Case Work Method in Social Work Evaluation*, Council on Social Work Education, New York.

Brodsky, Annette, M. (1981). "Planning for the Female Offender M.Q. Warren (ed.) *Comparing Female and Male Offenders*, American Society of Criminology, Beverty Hills, Sage Publications, London.

Bustsmante, D.H. (1975). "The Nature of Female Criminal", *Issues in Criminology*, Fall 8, 2, pp. 117-135.

Campbell, A. (1981). *Girl Delinquents*, Basil Blackwell, Oxford.

Campbell, A. (1984). *The Girls in the Gang: A Report from New York City*, Basil Blackwell, Oxford.

Carlen, P. (1983). *Women's Imprisonment*, Routledge and Kegan Paul, London.

Chadha, K. (1983). *The Indian Jail*, New Delhi, Vikas Publishing House Pvt. Ltd.

Chowdhry, Paul (1983). *Introduction to Social Work*, Atma Ram & Sons, Delhi.

Cohen, Albert K. (1955). *Delinquent Boys: The Culture of the Gang*, Glencoe, Ill, Free Press.

Cohen, Albert K. (1970). *Deviance and Control*, Prentice-Hall of India Pvt. Ltd., New Delhi.

Cohen, Lawrence E. & Land, Kenneth, C. (1987). Age Structure and Crime: Symmetry Versus Asymmetry and the Projection of Crime Rates through the 1990s, *American Sociological Review*, Vol. 52.

Compendium of Crime of Police Statistics of Tamil Nadu, (1988). *Crime in India*, 1983.

Cowie, J.V. & Eliot Slater et al. (1968). *Delinquent in Girls*, Hienemann Publishers, London.

Cowie, J., Cowie, V. & Slater, E. (1971). *Delinquent in Girls*, Hienemann Educational Books Ltd., London.

Cressey, D.R. (1971). "Delinquent and Criminal Structures", R.K. Merton and R. Nisbet (eds.) *Contemporary Social Problems*, 3rd ed. Harcourt Bruce, Jovanovich, New York.

Cressey, D.R. (1959). Professional Correctional Work and Professional Work in Correction, *National Probation and Parole Association Journal*, Vol. 3, No. 1.

Datesman, S.K. and Frank, R. Scarpritti, (1975). Female Delinquency and Broken Homes: A Restaurant, *Criminology* 13, May.

Datesman, S.K., F.R. Scarpritti & R.M. Stephenson, (1975). Female Delinquency; An Application of Self and Opportunity Theories, *Journal of Research in Crime and Delinquency,* 12 (2): 107-123.

Dateeman, S.K., Frank, R. Scarpritti, (1980). *Women, Crime and Justice,* Oxford University Press, New York.

Devasia V.V. and Leelamma Devasia, (1982). "Prison as a Treatment Institution", *Nagpur Times,* Nov. 9th.

Devasia, V.V. and L. Devasia (1984). "Socio-Cultural Background on Homicide and Prison Life: A Study of Life Term Prisoners". *Indian Journal of Criminology and Criminalists,* Vol. IV, Jan.-Apr. No. 1 & 2, pp. 5-8.

Devasia, V.V. and L. Devasia (1989). "Prison as a Social System and Prisonization in Relation to Prison Administration", *Indian Journal of Public Administration,* Vol. XXXIV, No. 1, pp. 144-51.

Lewis, D. (1981). Black Women Offenders and Criminal Justice: Some Theoretical Considerations, Warren, M. (ed). *Comparing Female and Male Offenders,* Sage Publications Inc., Baverly Hills.

Linz, M.C. (1986). *Women and Crime, The Female Offender,* Signs, Autumn, Vol. 12, pp. 78-96.

Lipton, D. Martison, R. and Wilks, J. (1976). *The Effectiveness of Correctional Treatment,* A Survey of Treatment Evaluation Studies, Prager Publication, New York.

Lombroso, Caser and F. William (1958). *The Female Offender,* Philosophical Library, New York.

Mala, M. (1960). "Problems of Women Offenders of Naribandi Niketan", Lucknow, *Journal of Correctional Work,* pp. 85-911.

Mangrum, C.T. (1976). *The Professional Practitioner in Probation*, Charles G. Thomas, Spring Field.

Mamby, R. (1980). "Sex and Crime: The Results of a Self-report Study, *British Journal of Sociology*, 31, 525.

Mazumdar, Sudha (1957). "Women in Prison at Home and Aboard", *Orient Longman*, Calcutta.

Menon, N.R. Madhava (1976). *Criminal Justice System in Relation to Women and Children, Some Issues and Perspectives*, Souvenir of VI Annual Conference of India, Society of Criminology.

Merton, R.K. (1957). *Social Theory and Social Structure*, (Rev. ed.), Free Press, Glencoe.

Merton, J.H. (1934). Female Homicides, *Journal of Mental Sciences*, Vol. LXXX.

Merton, Robert, K. (1968). *Social Theory and Social Structure*, Amrind Publishing Co. Pvt. Ltd., New Delhi.

Misra, Surat & J.C. Arora, (1982). *Crime Against Women*, Bureau of Police Research and Development, New Delhi.

Monger, M. (1972). *Case Work in Probation*, Butterworths, London.

Morris, Allison, (1987). *Women, Crime and Criminal Justice*, Basil Blackwell, New York.

Morris, A. and L. Gelsthrope (1981). "False Clues and Female Crime", In A. Morris and L. Gelsthrope (eds.), *Women and Crime*, Institute of Criminology, Cambridge.

Morris, R. (1964). Female Crime: The Construction of Women in Criminology, Allen and Unwin, London.

Naffine Nagaire, (1987). *Female Crime,* The Construction of Women in Criminology, Allen and Unwin, London.

Nagla, B.K. (1932). "The Criminality of Women in India",

Indian Journal of Social Work, Vol. 43," pp. 273-282.

Nagla, B.K. (1981). "The Juvenile Delinquents in Society", *Indian Journal of Criminology*, 9, 1 January, pp. 44-50.

Nagla, B.K. (1982). "The Criminality of Women in India" *Indian Journal of Social Work*, Vol. XLII, No. 3, October.

Nagla, B.K. (1985). Women and Crime: A Sociological Analysis of Women Criminality in India, The India *Journal of Criminology and Criminalistics*, Vol. V, No. 324, July, December, 1985.

Nagla, B.K. (1991). *Women, Crime and Law*, Rawat Publications, New Delhi.

National Commission of the Causes and Prevention of Violence (1969). U.S. Government Printing Office, Washington D.C. 847.

Nye, F.I. and J.F. Short, Jr. (1957). "Scaling Delinquency Behaviour", *American Sociological Review* 22 (3), pp. 326-331.

Pagelow, (1985). "Violent Husbands and Abused Wives: A Longituainal Study" in J. Pahl (ed). *Private Violence and Public Policy*, Routledge and Kegan Paul, London.

Paramguru Pon (1984). "Women and Crime", *Indian Journal of Criminology*, Vol. 12, No. 2, July.

Pollak, Otto (1950). *The Criminality of Women*, Philadelphia, The University of Pennsylania Press.

Pollak, Otto (1951). *The Criminality of Women*, The University of Pennsylania Press, 80.

Pollak, Otto (1959). *The Criminality of Women*, A.S. Barnes, New York.

Prasad, S.K.K. (1981). *A Study of Women Prisoners in Tamil Nadu*, Paper presented at the Tenth Annual Conference of Indian Society of Criminology, February, pp 13-15.

Prasad, S.K.K. (1982). *A Study of Women Murderers in Tamil Nadu, Readings in Criminology,* Sourvenir Volume, Indian Society of Criminology.

Price, Ray, R. (1977). *The Forgotten Female Offender, Crime and Delinquency,* 23 (2) pp. 101-108.

Punekar, S.D. and Rao, Kamala, (1962). *A Study of Prostitutes* in Bombay: With References to Family Background, Allied Publishers Pvt. Ltd., Bombay.

Rajan, V.N. (1981). "Role of Voluntary Organizations in Community Crime Prevention: *Indian Journal of Criminology and Criminalistics,* Vol. I, No. 2 & e, June-Sept.

Ramadevi, B.N. (1981). "Female Criminality: Causes and Consequences", Paper presented at the Tenth Annual Conference of the Indian Society of Criminology, Aurangabad, February.

Rani, Bilmoria, M. (1977). "A Report of Female Criminality in India", *Yojana,* April, 15.

Rani, Bilmoria, M. (1979). "Female Property Offenders in Andhra Pradesh", *Social Defence,* Vol. XIV, No. 55, January.

Rani, Bilmoria, M. (1981). "The Pattern and Nature of Female Criminality in Andhra Pradesh", *Indian Journal of Social Work,* Vol. XLI, No. 4, pp. 393-401.

Rani, Bilmoria, M. (1983). "Homicides by Females", *Indian Journal of Criminology,* Vol. 2, No. 1, pp. 8-17.

Rani, Bilmoria, M. (1987). "Female Criminality, Eastern in India", *Yojana,* April, 15.

Rao, S. Venugopal. (1967). "Murder" A Pilot Study of Urban Patterns with particulars Reference to Delhi, C.B.I. , New Delhi.

Rao, Venugopal, (1981). "Female Criminality". Paper presented at the Tenth Annual Conference of the Indian Society of Criminology, Aurangabad, February.

Reckless, Walter, C. Simon Dinitz, and Elten Murray, (1956). "Self-Concept as an Insulator against Delinquency", *American Sociological Review* 21 (December), pp. 744-746.

Reckless, Walter, C. Simon Dinitz, and Barbara Kay, (1957). "The Self Component in Potential Non-Delinquency". *American Sociological Review,* 22 (Oct.) pp. 566-570.

Reckless, W. and B. Kay (1967). *The Female Offender* (Consultant's Paper), President's Commission on Law Enforcement, Washingtonm DC, Mimeo.

Reckless, Walter, C. (1957). "Female Criminality", *National Probation and Parole Association Journal,* 3rd January, pp. 1-5.

Reckless, Walter, C. (1971). *The Crime Problem,* Vakils, Feffer and Simons Private Ltd., Bombay.

Reckless, Walter, C. Simon Dinitz, (1967). "Pioneering with Self-Concept as a Vulnerability Factore in Delinquency". *Journal of Criminal Law, Criminology and Police Science* 58 (December) 515-523.

Report of the All India Working Group on Prison Reforms, (1971-1973).

Report of the Prison Reforms Commission, Tamil Nadu (1978-1979).

Report of the National Expert Committee on Women Prisons, (1985-1986).

Report of the National Expert Committee on Women Prisons, (1987) Dept. of Women and Child Development, Ministry of Human Resources, 2 Volumes.

Roberts A.R. (Ed) (1974). *Correctional Treatment of the Offenders*, Charles C. Thomas, Spring Field.

Ronald L. Simons, & Martin G. Miller and Stephen M. Aigner, (1980). "Contemporary Theories of Deviance and Female Delinquency; An Empirical Test". *Journal of Research in Crime and Delinquency*.

Sanyal, S. (1974). "An Empirical Study of Certain Personality Characteristics and Attitudes of 25 Female Convicts of Nari Bandi Niketan", *Journal of Correctional Work*, No. xx, 70-82.

Sanyal, S. (1975). "An Empirical Study of Certain Personality Characteristics and Attitudes of 25 Female Convicts of Nari Bandi Niketan", *Social Defence*, Vol. XI, No. 41, July.

Sanyal & Vimal Agarwal, (1981). "Women Convict in Nari Bandi Niketan: An Integrated Approach". *Indian Journal of Criminology*, Vol. 9, No. 2.

Saraswati Mishra, (1985). "Rehabilitation of Women Prisoners", Indian Journal of Criminology, Vol. 13, No. 1, January.

Saxena, Rekha and Shukla, K.S. (1984). "Women and Crime: An Emerging Issue for Social Enquiry in India", *Indian Journal of Criminology and Criminalistics*, Vol. IV, No. 3 and 4.

Saxena, Rekha and S. Sanyal. (1989). "Rehabilitation Problems of Women Prisoners", *Indian Police Journal*, Vol. 36, No. 1, Jan.-March, pp. 33-39.

Saxena, Rekha (1994). *Women and Crime in India: A Study in Sociocultural Dynamics*, Inter-India Publications, New Delhi.

Schaker, Stephen (1969). *Theories in Criminology*, New York, Random House.

Scutt, Jocelynne, A. (1974). "A Factor in Female Crime", *The Criminologist*, Vol. 9, No. 34, pp. 56-71.

Scutt, Jocelynne, A. (1974). Perspectives (ed.), *The Other Side of Socio-Psychological Implications*, Sage Publications India Ltd., New Delhi.

Sharma, Madhu (1987). "Crime and Women: A Psychological Perspective", *Indian Journal of Criminology*, 15 (2) July, 126-30.

Shastri, Tara (1981). "Women Prisoners in Maharashtra State: A Socio-Economic Survey", *Social Defence*, XVII, 66, October.

Shubhdra Ghosh (1986). *Female Criminals in India, A Psychological Study of Inmates of Nari Bandi Niketan*, Uppal Publishing House, New Delhi.

Shukla, K.S. and Rekha Saxena, (1987). "Women and Crime: A Perspective" (ed.), *The Other side of Development: Socio-Psychological Implications*, Sage Publications India Ltd, New Delhi.

Sikka, K.D. (1985). "Social Work in Correctional Settings: An Analysis, (Ed.) "*Social Defence*" Vol. XXI, No. 82.

Sikka, K.D. (1985). "Offenders Against Life: Some Socio-Psychological Aspects, *The Indian Journal of Social Work*, Vol. XLVI, No. 2.

Sikka, K.D. (1986). "Women in Indian Prisons: Major Issues". *Indian Journal of Social Work*, Vol. XLVII, No. 2.

Simon, R. (1975). *Women and Crime*, D.C. Health and Co., Lexington.

Simons, L. Ronald, et al., (1980). "Contemporary Theories of Deviance and Female Delinquency—An Empirical Test", *Journal of Research in Crime and Delinquency*.

Singh, Arvinder, (1981) "Personality of Female Murderer", *Indian Journal of Criminology*, Vol. 9, No. 2, July.

Singh, M. (1980). "A Study of Personality of Murderers and the Psycho-Social Factors Related to Murder", *Indian Journal of Criminology*, 8, 1, 15-20.

Singh, M.K. (1981). "Women and Crime Phenomenon", *Indian Journal of Social Work*, Vol. XLII, No. 3, October, 1981, pp. 281-292.

Sivamurthy, A. (1987). "Crime Trend in Tamil Nadu", *Indian Journal of Criminology*, Vol. 15, No. 1.

Smart, Carol, (1976). *Women Crime and Criminology: A Feminist Critique*, Routledge and Kegan Paul, Bombay.

Smart, C. (1979). "The New Female Criminal: Reality and Myth? British? *Journal of Criminology*, 19, 1, 50.

Smith, A. (1962). *Women in Prison*, Stevans and Son, London.

Smith, Ann. D. (1962). Women Prisoners: Sexism Behind Bars, *Professional Psychology*, April,. 331.

Smith, N.K. (1974). "Women Prisoners", *Indian Journal of Social Work*, Vol. 35, No. 2, July, pp. 137-148.

Sohoni, N.K. (1989). *Women Behind Bars*, Vikas Publishing House, New Delhi.

Srivastava, S.P. (1974). "The Feel of Imprisonment: An Evaluation Study of the Impact of Incarceration of 400 Long-Term Prisoners of a Central Jail in U.P.", *Indian Journal of Criminology*.

Srivastava, S.P. (1975). "Social Work with Prisoners", *Social Work Forum*, Vol. 13.

Srivastava, S.P. (1975). "The Concept of Prison Community: A Theoretical Analysis", *Indian Journal of Criminology*, 3(1).

Srivastava, S.P. (1982). "Rehabilitation of Fallen Women and Girls Needs for a New Outlook" *Indian Journal of Criminology*, Vol. 10, No. 1.

Srivastava, S.P. (1984). "Women Crime and Criminal Justice System in India", *Indian Journal of Criminology and Criminalistics*, Vol. IV, No. 3 and 4, Sept.-Dec, 92-105.

Srivastava, S.P. (1989). *Juvenile Justice in India: Policy Programme and Perspectives*, Ajanta Publications, New Delhi.

Srivastava, T.N. (1985). *Women and the Law*, Intellectual Publishing House: New Delhi.

Steffensemeier, D. (1980). "Sex Differences in Patterns of Adult Crime: A Review and Assessment", *Social Forces*, Vol. 58, No. 4, pp. 1080-1108.

Sutherland, E.H. and Cressy, D.R. (1958). "Principles of Criminology" (6th ed.), *Times of India Press*, p. 7, Bombay.

Sutherland, Edwin. H. and Cressy Donald, R. (eds.) (1966). *Principles of Criminology* 7th, J.P, Lippincott, Philadelphia.

Sutherland, Edwin. H. and Cressy Donald, R. (1968). Principles of Criminology, (6th ed), The Times of India Press, Bombay.

Sutherland, E.H. and D.R. Cressy, (1978). *Criminology*, 10th ed. Philadelphia, Lippincott.

Sykes, G.M. (1956/1958). The Society of Captives, Princeton University Press, Princeton, N.J.

Tappan, P.W. (Ed.) (1951). *Contemporary Corrections*, McGraw Hill Book Company, Inc, New York.

Tappan, Paul (1960). *Crime, Justice and Corrections*, McGraw-Hill, New York.

The Economist, (1990-92). Crime in America, The *Economist Newspaper Ltd.*, London, Dec-Jan.

Thomas, W.I. (1907/1923/1967). *The Unadjusted Girl*, Harper and Row, New York.

Treger, Harvey et. al., (1974). "A Police-Social Work Team Model", *Crime and Deliquency.*

Trivedi, V.B. and K.P. Kriahna, (1983). "Murderer and Her Victim", *Indian Journal of Criminology,* Vol. II, No. 2, July, 115-118.

Turk (1971). *Criminality and Legal Order,* Chandler Publishing Company, Seranton.

United Nations (1955). *Standard Minimum Rules for the Treatment of Prisoners,* Report of the first U.N. Congress on the Prevention of Crime and Treatment of the Offender, Geneva.

Venter, Clyde B. and Dora B. Somerville, (1970.) *The Delinquent Girl.* Charles C. Thomas, Springfield; Illinois.

Visuvathas Jeya Singh, J. (1987). *Theories of Crime and Delinquency,* Deviant Children, Visuthamby Publishers, Madras.

West, D.J. (1967). *The Young Offender,* Penguin Books Ltd. , London.

William Thomas (1993). *Family and Crime,* Paper presented at the Annual Conference of ISSA, Coimbatore.

Wolfgang, M.E. (1958). *Patterns in Criminal Homicide,* Philadelphia.

Wolfgang, Marvin E. (1967). "A Sociological Analysis of Criminal Homicide in Marvin Wolfgang" (ed.) *Studies in Homicide,* Harper and Row, New York.

Young, P.V. (1977). *Scientific Social Surveys and Research,* Prentice-Hall of India Pvt. Ltd, New Delhi.

Appendices

APPENDIX-I
INTERVIEW SCHEDULE

WOMEN CRIMINALS IN TAMIL NADU

I. PERSONAL DATA

1. Name :
2. Age :
3. Education :
4. Marital Status :
5. Previous Occupation :
6. Caste :
7. Religion :
8. Income Per month (Before Sentencing) :
9. Native Place :

    a. Before Marriage :

        i. Rural / Urban   ii. Dist.______________

    b. After Marriage

        i. Rural / Urban   ii. Dist.______________

II. FAMILY BACKGROUND

A. Data on Family of Orientation

1. Family Particulars:

Sl. No.	*Relation to Resp.*	*Age*	*Edn.*	*Occn.*	*Income*	*Presently at (R/U)*
1.	Father					
2.	Mother					
3.	Brother(s)					
4.	Sister(s)					
5.	G. Parents(s)					

2. Type of Family a. Nuclear b. Joint Family
3. You have been brought by whom
   a. Parents b. Grand Parents
   c. Relatives d. Others (Specify):
4. If you brought by other than your parents their
   i. Education :
   ii. Occupation :

B. School Drop Out

1. Whether you were a drop out from the school?
   Yes / No
2. If yes, what are the reasons?
3. If drop out what were the activities you engaged?
   a. Keeping Idel b. Child labour
   c. Helping in the family affairs d. Others (Specify):

C. Parental Treatment and Residence Description

1. Did your Parent / Guardian treat all the children alike?
   Yes / No.

2. If no, did you feel any preferential treatment between boys and girls? Yes / No.
3. Description about the residence where the respondent grown up.
   - i. With over Crowding Yes / No
   - ii. With narrow rooms Yes / No
   - iii. With lack of space Yes / No
   - iv. In a poverty condition Yes / No
   - v. Conflicting nature of Parents/Guardian Yes / No
   - vi. Quarrelsome nature of Parents/Guardian Yes / No
   - vii. Chances of exposure to Criminal Risk Yes / No
4. If conflict existed the reasons are:

   a. Poverty b. Unemployment c. Alcoholism

   d. Adultery e. Misbehaviour f. Others (Specify):

D. Childhood Criminal Behaviour:

1. Whether you involve in Criminal activity along with your parent or guardian? Yes / No
2. If yes, Whether you were trained? Yes / No
3. Whether your childhood playmates have criminal record? Yes / No
4. Whether any of your close relative have criminal record? Yes / No

E. Data on Family of Procreation

(If married additional questions)

1. Place of Marriage
2. Whether the husband's caste is

   a. Same or b. different

3. Particulars of the family of procreation:

Sl.No.	Relation to Resp.	Age	Edn.	Occn.	Income	Presently at (R/U)

4. Whether it is the first marriage for you? Yes / No
5. Whether it is the first marriage for your husband? Yes / No
6. If no, give marriage particulars:

		Husband	Respondent
Age at Marriage	i. First Marriage		
	ii. Second Marriage		
	iii. Third Marriage		

7. Whether the marriage the last one is a:

   a. Love Marriage b. Arranged Marriage

8. Whether the respondent was as a:

   a. Concubine b. Mistress

F. Relationship with Husband and Others

1. Whether any illegal relationship exists for

   a. Husband Yes / No

   b. Respondent Yes / No

2. Did you face conflict with you husband? Yes / No

3. If yes, what are the reasons

   i. Poverty ii. Unemployment iii. Adultery

   iv. Drunkenness v. Others Specify

4. Did you experience any illtreatment from your

   a. Husband Yes / No

   b. Parent-in Law Yes / No

   c. In-Laws Yes / No

   d. Relatives Yes / No

5. What are the type of illtreatment?

6. What are the reasons for illtreatment?

G. Details of Husband

1. Whether your husband employed? Yes / No

2. If yes, what is the occupation.

3. What is the nature of occupation?

4. Income of the Husband:

5. Whether your Husband:

   i. Had illegal relationship Yes / No

   ii. Is an alcoholic Yes / No

   iii. Is a drug addict Yes / No

   iv. Affected by chronic illness Yes / No

   v. Involved in Criminal activity Yes / No

6. Where is your Husband at present:

H. Employment of Respondent

(If the respondent was employed before sentencing)

1. What was the occupation?

2. What is the nature of occupation?

3. Whether any shift in the occupation? Yes / No

4. If yes, the reasons for shifting are

   a. Illtreatment of the empolyer b. Less Salary

   c. No Satisfaction d. Others (Specify):

5. Relationship to the employer

   a. Very Cordial b. Cordial c. Normal

   d. Less Cordial e. Hartred.

6. Role of the respondents in her family (of procreation is married)

   a. Earning member b. Only bread winner

   c. House Wife d. Financial Manager

   e. Dependent

III. CRIME COMMITTED:

A. Details of Crime:

1. What was the crime committed?
2. Where it was committed? Dist.:
3. When it was committed? Year:
4. Why it was committed?

B. Acceptance of Crime:

1. Do you accept the crime? Yes / No
2. If yes, under what circumstances it was committed?
3. If no, whether false implication has been done? Yes / No
4. If yes, who had falsely implicated?
5. What are the reasons for false implication?

C. Enquiry for Murderers:

1. Who was the victim:
2. What are the reasons for murdering?
3. Whether it involved accomplice(s)? Yes / No

4. If yes, the role of the respondent in the crime is

   a. Main Role b. Subsidiary Role

5. If it involves accomplice(s) the accomplice(s) is/are

   i. Husband ii. Brother iii. Sister

   iv. Relatives (Specify): v. Others (Specify)

6. Your relation to the victim:
7. What was the weapons used?

D. Enquiry for Non - Murderers:

1. Whether your criminal behaviour resulted in physical harms to the victim? Yes / No
2. If yes, Who was the victim
3. Whether the physical harm is

   a. Major or b. Minor

4. Whether your crime involves any property loss to the victim? Yes / No
5. If yes, the worth of the property: Rs.
6. And who was the victim:
7. Whether your crime involved loss to the Govt.?

   Yes / No

8. Whether your crime involved loss to the people?

   Yes / No

9. Whether you have done a crime related to drug?

   Yes / No

10. Whether crime related to illicit distillation?

    Yes / No

11. Whether your criminal behaviour resulted in loss of moral turpitude? Yes / No
12. If yes, how did you get into the profession?

13. Whether the crime was done
    a. Alone b. With an accomplice
14. If with an accomplice
    i. The role of the respondent
    a. Main Role b. Subsidiary
    ii. The accomplice is:

1. As soon as you have done the crime whether you try to
   a. Escape b. Surrender to the Police
2. If surrendered—Why you did so?
3. What is your reaction as soon as you have
4. What do your feel about it at present

Particulars of Juvenile Record (If any):

Sl.No.	*Crime Committed*	*Age*	*Reasons*	*Apprehension Details Period & Place)*

Particulars of Adult Criminal Record (If any):

Sl.No.	*Crime Committed*	*Age*	*Reasons*	*Apprehension Details (Period & Place)*

1. List out the cause for criminal activity:

a. Poverty

b. Unemployment

c. Economic Responsibility

d. Very low salary

e. Too many children

f. To earn more money

g. To lead a luxury life

h. Illegal relationship of the respondent

i. Illegal relationship of the husband

j. Illtreatment of the husband

k. Illtreatment of the relatives

l. Drunkenness of the husband

m. Illtreatment at the work place

n. Emotional reasons

o. Self defence (Against raping etc.,)

p. Escape from thieves

q. Attrocities of high caste people

r. Don't know

s. Others (Specify)

IV. CONSEQUENCE OF CRIME

A. On the Individual

Sl. No.	*Statements*	*Fully Agree*	*Agree*	*Neutral*	*Dis-Agree*	*Fully Agree*
1.	Due to Crime academic life					
2.	Crime involves financial loss					
3.	Social Status has been affected					
4.	Personal life has been affected					
5.	Individual freedom is affected					
6.	Criminals feel depressed					
7.	Criminals feel detached from the family					
8.	Criminals often get self anger					
9.	Criminals feel detached from the entire society.					

B. On the Children

Sl. No.	*Statements*	*Fully Agree*	*Agree*	*Neutral*	*Dis Agree*	*Fully Agree*
1	*2*	*3*	*4*	*5*	*6*	*7*
1.	Children's upbringing is a problem.					
2.	Irreparable loss to the children					
3.	Children's education is the problem					
4.	Children's personality affected					

1	2	3	4	5	6	7
5.	Children loss moral support					
6.	A negative model to the Children					
7.	Loss control over Children					
8.	Children face social harassment					
9.	Children may expose to criminal risk					
10.	Mother is the most important factor in children's upbringing					

C. On the Family

Sl. No.	*Statements*	*Fully Agree*	*Agree*	*Neutral*	*Dis Agree*	*Fully Agree*
1.	Parent (in law) feel mental agony					
2.	Economic loss to the family					
3.	Family face social harassment					
4.	Status of the family affected					
5.	A negative model to siblings					
6.	Irreparable loss to the husband / Parents					
7.	Marriage life is a problem					
8.	Siblings future life affected					
9.	Neighour's relation-ship affected					
10.	Leads to disintegration of family					

D.On the Society

Sl. No.	Statements	Fully Agree	Agree	Neutral	Dis-Agree	Fully Agree
1.	Criminals feel that they have done much harm to the society					
2.	Criminals know that their activity resulted in loss to the Government					
3.	Criminals understand that their activity resulted in loss to the Government					
4.	Resulted in Law and Order problem					
5.	Criminal behaviour lessens participation in social activities					
6.	Criminal behaviour influence neighbour negatively					
7.	Criminal behaviour lessens political participation					
8.	Criminal behaviour lessens religious participation					
9.	Criminals sown seeds to problematic society					
10.	The Society gets polluted					

V. Prison Life

A. Level of Satisfaction Regarding the Facilities in Prison:

Sl. No.	*Facilities*	*Highly Satisfied*	*Satisfied*	*Neutral*	*Dissatisfied*	*Fully Dissatisfied*
1.	Food:					
	i. Breakfast					
	ii. Lunch					
	iii. Dinner					
2.	Accommodation					
3.	Bathing					
4.	Clothing					
5.	Medical Facilities					
6.	Recreation					
7.	Other Welfare Facilities					
8.	Educational Facilities					
9.	Vocational Training					
10.	Work / Labour					
11.	Incentive (if any)					
12.	Grievance redressal					
13.	Relationship with fellow inmates					
14.	Communication Facilities					
15.	Treatment by the staff					

B. General Information

1. Period of Punishment:
2. Whether your husband (if married) visiting you?
   Yes / No
3. If yes, how often in a month
4. Whether your relations visiting you? Yes / No
5. If yes, how often in a month
6. What are the difficulties you face in the prison?
   Yes / No
7. Whether the prison life
   a. Helped b. Harmed you?
8. If (a) in what ways
   i. Change of behaviour
   ii. Change of criminal attitude
   iii. Vocational training
   iv. Others (Specify):
9. If (b) in what ways
   i. Development of more criminal attitude
   ii. Punishment rather that rehabilitation oriented
   iii. Environment is harmful
   iv. Others (Specify):
10. Any rotation system available in the prison? Yes / No
11. If yes, what are the assignment give:
12. Whether you are given any special responsibility or post give details:
13. Do you feel that your personality has been improved?
    Yes / No

14. How do you feel about the prison life in general?
15. Given your suggestions to improve the present condition in the prison

    a. b.

    c. d.

    e.

VI. FUTURE PLANS

1. After your release:

    (i). Where would you like to go?

    (ii). What would you like to do?

    a. Own Business b. House Wife

    c. Try for job d. Others (Specify):

    (iii). What type of difficulties you face

    a. Economical b. Personal

    c. Familial d. Children

    e. Employment f. Others (Specify):

2. Do you feel that your family will accept you? Yes / No
3. Do you feel that the society will accept you? Yes / No
4. What is your idea regarding the attitudes of the society towards you?
5. What kind of help expect from the Government?

    a. Financial b. Guidance

    c. Training d. Employment

    e. Others (Specify) :

6. Will you assure yourself that you do not commit crime in the future ? Yes / No

APPENDIX - II

TABLE 1

CRIME DATA FOR SELECTED COUNTRIES

Countries	*Year*	*Volume of Crime per 100,00 population*	*Total Offenders*	*Female Offenders as % of total*
Australia	1980	8044.96	209707	12.50
Canada	1980	11534.62	1014333	09.50
France	1980	4903.07	686354	17.34
India	1977	202.46	1538515	01.90
Japan	1980	1293.59	551577	18.50
United Kingdom (England & Wales)	1980	5458.98	555257	17.00
U.S.A.	1980	5900.00	10441000	17.00

Source: Interpol, International Crime Statistics, 1979-80, pp. 6, 23, 49, 57, 64, 78, 123.
International Criminal Police Organisation, International Crime Statistics, 1979-80, Saint Cloud, France, IOPO, International General Secretariat.

TABLE 2

CRIME-WISE DISTRIBUTION OF PERSONS ARRESTED UNDER IPC (1980- 88)

Crime	1980		1981		1982		1983		1984		1985		1986		1987		1988	
	Male	Female	Male	Female	Male	Female	Male	Female	Male	Female	Male	Female	Male	Female	Male	Female	Male	Female
Murder	2978	173	3070	127	3534	127	2015	98	3021	34	3025	157	3446	161	3224	209	3353	184
Culpable Homicide	0015	--	0012	--	0024	--	0028	--	0003	02	0010	002	0019	--	0052	--	0070	005
Rape	0183	001	0225	--	0232	--	0250	02	0281	--	0331	002	0312	--	0339	005	0394	003
Kidnapping & Abduction	0625	022	0697	019	0788	023	0780	22	0813	10	0817	048	1056	059	0783	073	0966	073
Dacoity	0251	002	0626	--	0147	002	0203	--	0205	--	0201	--	0255	002	0213	--	0243	--
Robbery	0314	003	0442	002	0319	001	0494	03	0501	181	0480	004	0585	004	0550	001	0557	001
Burglary	5459	089	5907	098	8973	100	7169	93	5882	185	5654	118	5271	036	5022	049	4737	055
Theft	10647	702	19926	625	17974	500	22541	791	18308	1323	19432	716	17013	583	14015	503	14851	506
Riots	59645	1922	63301	1669	55289	3041	48338	2199	52516	0776	71414	6650	57600	2986	66479	5345	00456	3007
Criminal breach of trust	0662	008	0712	004	0859	010	0996	013	0812	064	0568	017	0618	019	0521	008	0585	013
Cheating	0491	013	0894	011	0721	022	1056	22	0816	057	0599	009	0822	031	0980	092	0891	024
Counter feiting	0064	001	0104	--	0109	--	0095	--	0105	--	0093	--	0110	001	0083	001	0071	--

Source : Adopted from compendium of Police and Crime Statistics of Tamil Nadu 1980-88.

TABLE 3

PERSONS AFFECTED UNDER LOCAL AND SPECIAL ACTS DURING 1986—88

Local and special acts	*1986*			*1987*			*1988*		
	Male	*Female*	*Percentage of female*	*Male*	*Female*	*Percentage of female*	*Male*	*Female*	*Percentage of female*
Areas Act	176		—	110	—	—	193	—	—
Opium Act	070	—	—	809	143	15.02	1372	144	09.49
Gambling	46952	545	01.41	46108	375	00.80	46373	174	00.37
Excise	002	—	—	001	—	—	001	—	—
Prohibition	65568	8588	11.58	185236	27147	12.78	310610	30165	08.85
Explosives / Explosive Substances Act	341	—	—	259	003	01.16	427	004	00.94
S.I.T.A	272	8743	96.98	049	8292	99.41	941	8112	89.67
Customs	020	006	23.07	032	—	—	—	—	—
Indian Raliways Act	065	—	—	042	—	—	025	—	—
Other offenders local & special acts	389610	31924	07.57	4039061	19193	04.53	—	—	—

Source: Adapted from the Crime and Police Statistics of Tamil Nadu 1986-88.

TABLE 4

NUMBER OF PERSONS ARRESTED BY SEX INTERMS OF INDEX WITH REFERENCE TO BASE YEAR 1971

Sex	*Year*													
	1971	*1972*	*1973*	*1974*	*1975*	*1976*	*1977*	*1978*	*1979*	*1980*	*1981*	*1982*	*1973*	*1984*
Male	100	129	148	132	132	90	142	195	203	231	252	242	237	221
Female	100	163	233	191	191	151	204	362	219	476	338	393	619	839

Source: Adapted from the Crime and Police statistics of Tamil Nadu 1971—84.

TABLE 5

PERSONS CHARGE SHEETED AND CONVICTED UNDER SITA IN TAMIL NADU IN 1979—88

Charge sheeted or Convicted	*Year*									
	1979	*1980*	*1981*	*1982*	*1983*	*1984*	*1985*	*1986*	*1987*	*1988*
Charge sheeted	6850	8450	9667	8915	9218	7894	9392	8995	8758	9868
Convicted	5452	8394	8638	8602	8891	7059	9256	8358	8345	8595

Source: Adapted from the Crime and Police statistics of Tamil Nadu 1979—88.

TABLE 6

PERSONS ARRESTED BY SEX UNDER IPC IN TAMIL NADU

Year	*Total No. of Persons arrested*	*Male arrested*	*Percentage of male to the total*	*Female arrested*	*Percentage of female to the total*
1978	137858	132998	96.47	4860	03.54
1979	142028	139079	97.92	2949	02.08
1980	164146	157769	92.12	6377	03.88
1981	176587	172057	97.43	4530	02.57
1982	170642	165369	96.90	8306	03.10
1983	17401	162095	95.12	8306,	04.88
1984	161717	150471	93.04	11246	06.96
1985	215454	200913	93.25	14541	06.75
1986	196561	187482	95.38	9079	04.62
1987	204485	194986	93.35	9499	04.65
1988	201976	189130	93.63	12846	06.37

Source: Adapted from the *Crime and Police Statistics of Tamil Nadu* 1978-88.

Index

❑❑❑